Dead Drunk

Saving myself from alcoholism in a Thai monastery

Paul Garrigan

PUBLISHED BY MAVERICK HOUSE PUBLISHERS

Maverick House Publishers, Office 19, Dunboyne Business Park,
Dunboyne, Co. Meath, Ireland.

info@maverickhouse.com
http://www.maverickhouse.com

ISBN: 978-1-905379-69-9

5 4 3 2 1

The paper used in this book comes from wood pulp of managed forest.
For every tree felled, at least one tree is planted, thereby renewing natural
resources.

A CIP catalogue record for this book is available from the British Library,
and Irish copyright libraries.

DEDICATION

To my father, who always tried his best.

ACKNOWLEDGEMENTS

I would like to thank the monks and volunteers at Wat Thamkrabok and everyone else who has tried to help me over the years.

CHAPTER 1

RIDING ALONG ON my motorbike, I watched as the Thai countryside awoke around me in the early morning light. I was nearing the end of this journey, and I was ready to embark on the next. After so many failed attempts to escape my addiction, I knew that now I was finally free from alcoholism. I had been a slave to alcohol for most of my life, and I couldn't wait to put this dependence behind me and start my life anew. As I sped further along, getting nearer to home, my mind was awhirl with plans and ideas, memories and remorse, hopes and fears.

The rainy season had just begun and there was plenty of work to do on the land. Groups of workers were gathering on the edge of paddy fields, laughing and starting their long day of labour cheerfully. I rode past these early risers, taking heart in their good humour.

Further on, I passed a number of orange-robed monks on their way back to the temples. They had just finished their morning alms round, and the sight of them filled me with gratitude, as it was their fellow monks who had just helped me break the cycle of self-destruction and despair. It was a privilege to witness these holy men carrying out a tradition that went back over two and a half thousand years.

Motorbikes whizzed by me in the opposite direction ferrying children to school, some carrying as many as five people. Everyone looked so full of life. I overtook motorbikes that looked as though they were about to fall apart, carrying impossibly heavy loads, but these expert riders managed to keep everything on board.

My recently sobered mind felt like it was waking up to the world for the first time in years. I felt as though I had acquired new powers of observation and perception. Colours, sounds and smells were all sharper and more vibrant now. The world seemed like an exciting place to be, full of possibilities. I could now see Thailand in a way that had previously eluded me, and I relished in the glory of that morning. I felt comradeship with every person I passed; we were all in it together, just struggling through life, doing our best. I was no better or worse than anybody else. I took in the wonder of the world all around me, and I felt excited and grateful to be able to witness it all.

I WAS ABOUT to start a new chapter in my life. Things had been bad for years, and I hoped that life would now take me in a new direction. This had to work. The thought of returning to my old way of living frightened me. If that were to happen, I was certain that I would not live for much longer. I had been addicted to alcohol for 20 years but I couldn't face another day of it—I would rather die.

My thoughts turned to my girlfriend, Oa; I had promised to return to her a new man. Upon entering the temple, I knew this promise needed to be more than just a pathetic cliché, or we would be finished. I couldn't continue to ruin her life as well as my own; she deserved more than that.

It felt like I had been away for much longer than a mere ten days. The wreck of a man who entered Thamkrabok temple was no more. Desperation had given way to hope; self-pity and self-loathing were now replaced with aspiration and an excitement about what the future might hold. As the moment when I would be reunited with Oa drew nearer and nearer, I wondered how she would react to my transformation. Would she even notice the major changes which seemed so obvious to me? I dreaded the thought that she might be suspicious and see it all as being too good to be true. Hadn't I let her down so many times before?

MAKING MY WAY down the central Thai highway, I had plenty of time for reflection. I wondered what my friends were doing back in Thamkrabok. I guessed the time to be nearly eight o'clock, so they would have just finished their morning dose of herbal tea. I could imagine *Matt's* face grimacing as he once again complained that it tasted disgusting. I missed the friends I'd made during recovery, and envied their safe temple routine, but that was behind me now. I was moving forward.

My mind returned to thoughts of how things were going to be different this time. My previous attempts at escaping addiction had all failed, and I had always been able to furnish these failures with any number of excuses—I wasn't ready at the time, I had forgotten the pain of addiction, it was normal for an addict to relapse, I was too young, life was too difficult—the list was endless. Failure was not an option now—this was my last chance.

When I first arrived at the temple, a Swiss monk told me to make good use of my time there. As well as detoxifying my body there was other work to be done. One of the most important tasks was to find out why I had ended up in such a desperate state and what direction my life was going to take once I left. The temple routine provided plenty of opportunity for thinking about these things. I began to look back on where I had gone wrong. When had my life first turned down the path of addiction? At first, I thought that maybe it had all started to go wrong in my teens, but on reflection, I realised this wasn't true. The seed had been planted long before that. I began to think that maybe my journey to the temple had begun as far back as my memory could reach.

CHAPTER 2

THE MEMORIES OF my life up until about the age of fourteen are only available to me in snatches; certain episodes can appear clear to me, but the days prior and subsequent to these events are missing. It is sometimes difficult to put these incidents into any type of order. The reason why my mind can easily retrieve certain images and not others does not seem to be connected to the significance of the memory. One of my aunties swears that I once chased her around the house with an axe, but I can't remember a thing about it. Yet, I can easily remember a lonely afternoon spent reading a comic book from that same period.

More so than images, however, when my mind turns to those early years, it is feelings which I readily remember—feelings of happiness, but also feelings of awkwardness. I often felt a little out-of-step with those around me. I imagined that everyone else knew some vital piece of information that they were keeping from me. Other people seemed to instinctively know how the world worked, and I envied the way that they manoeuvred through life more skilfully than I did. I never knew how to react to people, and this always left me feeling like an outsider. At seven, I was too young to realise that this is how many people feel at least occasionally.

Take football, for example. My cousins and I would watch matches together on television every Saturday afternoon with my grandad Joe. My family and I were living with my grandparents at the time until we got a place of our own. I enjoyed reading football comics but found the real thing boring. I knew that it was important to those around me that I liked the game, and so I would feign interest for the sake of fitting in, all the time praying for the match to end so that I could get back to my comics.

My cousins, however, had no difficulty in mustering enthusiasm for whatever match we happened to be watching, and this pleased my grandfather no end. They would make all the right remarks, and grandad would get into grown-up discussions with them, but he never spoke to me like an adult. I'd always manage to say the wrong thing, and would be given looks of bewilderment from him, or sometimes even the cutting comment: 'What's he fucking saying?' This would make my cousins howl with laughter and would lead to a barrage of mockery from them.

I knew my observations weren't being received well, but I'd continue to talk in the futile hope that the next thing I'd say would somehow regain my credibility. Eventually my prattle would become so annoying that my grandad would expel me to the kitchen to sit with the women. I would sit there on a small children's stool, feeling self-conscious, reading my *Roy of the Rovers* comics. The women would remark that it was odd that I liked to read so many football comics, yet had so little interest in the real thing; I had no explanation to offer them.

In a bid to earn some respect, I tried to join our local football team. St Joe's had a great reputation in Dublin, and even my grandad was impressed when he heard that I was to be given a try-out. My cousins were incredulous, however. They couldn't understand why anyone would want me on their football team but the truth was that I, unlike my cousins, lived in the local area and that was the only reason they let me try out. Besides, it was only the junior team.

My family came along to support my debut with St Joe's. I had completely failed to impress anybody at my first practice session, but I was given the chance to play in goal for this friendly match. Our side was doing well but most of the action was at the opposite end of the pitch and I soon became bored with my lack of participation. So, when another kid who had been watching from the sidelines came over for a chat, I saw him as welcome company. One thing led to another and I ended up leaving my post to pick blackberries with my new friend. This decision marked the end of any football career I might have had. My father was furious, while my grandfather didn't appear in the least surprised, and my cousins thought the whole thing was hilarious. It was this propensity for stupid decisions that made me feel like such an outsider. When others pointed out the oddness in my behaviour I could clearly see what they meant. The problem was that I felt unable to stop myself. I would get strange notions in my head and just go along with them.

Nevertheless, despite sometimes feeling silly and uneasy around other people, I was generally a happy child. I would become absorbed in my imagination, and the stories I read in children's books fuelled my daydreams. Sometimes, I would be fortunate enough to get other children to join me in my make-believe world, or I would join them in theirs, and these were very happy times for me. At home, however, things weren't always quite so good.

My parents argued often, and I hated it. There was never any physical violence, but the shouting used to terrify me. The only way that I could block these shouting matches out was by hiding and rolling myself into a ball. I would remain like this, terrified, until the shouting stopped. These arguments would usually end with my father storming out of the house, banging the front door as he went.

WHEN I WAS SEVEN years old, I was knocked down by a car and I had to spend three weeks in hospital. I loved being the centre of attention, and having other children on the ward to play with. I didn't miss school one bit; I considered watching television to be a far more enjoyable way to spend my time. Some of the things I saw in the hospital did scare me a little, but, overall, hospital was a fun place for me. I even began to enjoy the Lucozade drink that all my visitors seemed to bring when they came to visit. But the best thing about being in hospital was that nobody argued with me, or with each other.

I missed the peace and all the attention when I returned home, and after a few months I decided to try to return to the ward. I began complaining of intense abdominal pain and kicked up such a fuss that I was once again admitted to hospital. This time the doctors were at a loss to find the cause of my symptoms. They began to suspect that I was faking it but they decided to take out my appendix anyway, just to be on the safe side. It was only when the nurses scrubbed me for surgery that I told them I was feeling better. They were sceptical about my miraculous recovery but they discharged me the same day. I left with the warning that any more pain and it would be straight to the operating room. I decided that faking illness was not a very clever idea.

This hospital incident may have been a sign of things to come but I have realised that it is easy to reinterpret the past to fit in with what we know today; if I had become a high achiever, I might be looking back at the same events and seeing the seeds of my success there. Still, even during those early days, I was willing to take desperate measures to escape the realities of my life. Perhaps my journey to Thamkrabok began then.

CHAPTER 3

I WAS FASCINATED with alcohol from the moment I knew of its existence. I saw how it completely altered those around me. Adults, who were usually a bit moody and far too busy with grown-up things to spend time with us kids, would come alive when they had a few pints inside them. Once the effects of the alcohol kicked in, they would play football in the garden, joke around, and better still, give us money to buy crisps and lemonade. A few bottles of Guinness or Harp lager and they would be singing songs, or telling funny stories, and sometimes they got so drunk that they would make complete fools of themselves by falling over or saying something ridiculous. This making a fool of yourself seemed to be a really grown-up thing to do and was accepted by all the other adults with the words: 'You can't blame people for letting their hair down once in a while.'

The Ireland that I was raised in during the seventies and eighties was centred on alcohol and the pub; getting drunk seemed to be an expression of our national identity. I grew up with the notion that the Irish were famous for their love of a pint of Guinness and having the craic, and this was something for us Irish to be proud of. I looked at the adults around me and observed that a pint was both a reward for a job well done, and a way to ease the pain of life's disappointments. Alcohol was used both to celebrate and to drown one's sorrows. Of course there were also the drunks who scared me, but as my non-drinking grandmother might have pointed out: 'Some people just don't know when to stop.'

My parents weren't big drinkers. My mother would only have a couple of bottles of Smithwicks at the weekend, and she'd be tipsy after just a few sips. My father worked away from home most weekdays, so I don't know what he drank then but at the weekends he would have around three or four pints, and he never got drunk. He warned me of the dangers of alcohol, and seemed to fear that I would develop a taste for it. His own father had liked to drink alcohol a bit too much, and somebody once told him that alcoholism skipped a generation. This was enough for him to view any interest I showed towards alcohol with great suspicion, which he usually accompanied with a lecture.

Still, there were plenty of others who seemed to be having a great time on the booze. I loved hearing stories about the crazy things adults got up to while under the influence. These stories took on a mythological element for me and formed the backdrop to my youth. The message they instilled in me was that doing something particularly stupid when you'd had a few drinks could make you the centre of attention for weeks afterwards. It was almost heroic.

IT WAS AROUND this time that I experienced my first taste of alcohol. On this particular day, my friend had come around to play and we were alone in the sitting room. It was a Sunday and all the men of the family had gone to the pub, leaving us children alone with the women, who were busy preparing Sunday lunch in the kitchen. Sometimes, the men would bring us along to the pub, which I loved, but my father always moaned that a bar was no place for children. At the time, I thought he was such a spoilsport for saying that.

I had always been fascinated by two miniature bottles of alcohol which were kept over my grandparent's fireplace. My grandad had often assured me that one bottle contained real Guinness and the other contained real Harp, just like the labels promised. I wasn't sure if he was joking or not; sometimes it was hard to tell when adults were messing around. My grandparents always shouted at us kids if we went near the miniatures, but this only increased our interest in them.

My friend and I decided that, as we were alone in the sitting room, and free of our usual adult supervision, we should use the opportunity to find out what was actually inside these bottles. We had experimented with smoking earlier that day too by lighting pieces of paper rolled into cigarette shapes, but that just left us feeling queasy and we were ready to try something else. However, even at our young age we knew that if there actually was alcohol inside the miniatures, it wouldn't be enough to get a gnat drunk, but we still wanted to taste the stuff to find out why the adults loved it so much.

The mini bottles had tiny caps on them and we had to use our teeth to remove them. This turned out to be quite tricky, and I almost broke a tooth, but we managed eventually. We got just a sip out of each bottle, and the taste was completely vile. I don't know if this was because they were really out-of-date having been on the mantelpiece for years, or if this is how alcohol tastes to everyone the first time. Either way, it tasted disgusting, but we both pretended to like it. We even tried to convince each other that we were feeling a bit tipsy from the tiny bit of alcohol we had consumed. It would be another couple of years, however, before I'd have my first proper taste of drink—one Christmas when I was nine years old.

MY PARENTS AND I were visiting my aunts and uncles in Rathmichael in Co. Dublin. I really liked going there because there was always a lot of laughter and excitement in the house. Their overgrown garden seemed to be full of hidden treasures, like an abandoned car, and a big hole in the ground covered by a door; there was an air of mystery about the place and I found it very exciting. They also had a fascinating book collection which they kept on a small shelf in their sitting room. The titles of these books seemed very exotic to me as a child and I would stare at them for hours wondering what they could possibly be about.

On that Christmas morning, a couple of my uncles allowed me a sip from their cans of lager. I made the most of this until I found an almost full can which had been forgotten about. I drank all of it and when it was finished I found some more forgotten cans. I was soon feeling the effects of my alcohol intake and I ended up being very sick. When we left that evening, my father realised I had been drinking. He was furious, and he didn't go easy on me even though I was ill.

AT AROUND THIS time a new drink was launched on the market which was all the rage among the grown-ups, who were encouraged to drink this in the pub if they were driving—'pretend beer', or alcohol-free lager as it was more commonly known. To my mind, these new drinks were ideal for aspiring drinkers like myself. Every time we were brought to a pub I would nag my parents into buying me one. After all, they were basically alcohol free. Another of my favourites was Shandy that you bought in a can. Even though it only contained a tiny amount of alcohol, it was enough for me to convince myself that I could feel its effects.

I enjoyed sitting in pubs with the grown-ups, pretending that I was drinking beer like them. I would feel proud to have a bottle in front of me. I'd imagine myself becoming drunk and would watch the adults for clues as to how I should behave, trying to imitate them. Sometimes I went a bit over the top by laughing hysterically or swaying from side to side on my way to the toilet. While my friends were pretending to be soldiers or pirates, I was pretending to be a drunk.

In spite of all this, it would be outrageous to suggest that my early years were all about my waiting until I could get my hands on real alcohol. There was a lot more to my life than this. For instance, I loved books and I used to spend hours writing stories or making my own comic books. I also loved the Beatles, who were a bit old-fashioned even then, but my parents' record collection kept them alive for me. I wanted to join a band just like them when I was older and I took this ambition quite seriously at the time.

I desperately wanted to learn the guitar and went around all the houses near my grandparents' asking if there was anyone who could teach me how to play. My efforts were rewarded when a nearby musician taught me a few chords on his electric guitar.

My sincerity and dedication in wanting to learn convinced my father that it wasn't just a fad, so he bought me a proper guitar and arranged for me to have lessons at Blackrock College in Dublin. Nevertheless, despite my longing to become a musician, it soon became apparent to my family and friends, and years later to me, that I had no real talent. Still, it gave me a lot of enjoyment, and, I suppose, it was a healthier way of spending my time than pretending to be a drunk.

CHAPTER 4

IN MY TEENAGE years I developed an interest in martial arts. Although Bruce Lee had died a few years earlier, the excitement he had generated was still being felt in my part of the world. He used his fighting expertise to beat all the bad guys; who wouldn't want to be just like him? Video recorders weren't common at this time because they were still relatively expensive and most of our parents couldn't afford one, but we occasionally got to see his movies on film projectors in school or the local youth club halls. Most of my interest in martial arts, however, stemmed from reading about Bruce Lee in magazines and comics. The television series *Kung-Fu* also intrigued me and I was eager to learn a martial art.

I was a weedy kid, but I escaped being bullied by making the older boys laugh. I would earn whatever limited respect I could by giving the teachers cheek, or by verbally abusing the less popular kids. This strategy worked for me most of the time and, except for the occasional kicking after school, I had it fairly easy. Still, I felt uncomfortable in my skinny frame, and I wanted to be able to defend myself in a fight, to kick the tough guy's ass, just like Bruce Lee.

Karate was the first martial art I attempted. We had moved out of my grandparents' house and were now living in Shankill in south Dublin, and I found classes taking place in a local school. I threw myself into the fighting without reserve and spent all my free time practising the new moves I was learning. Soon, my body began to show the results of these efforts, and I experienced the natural high that comes from being physically fit. Unlike my attempts to learn the guitar, this felt like something I could really master with a little work and effort.

My father was impressed by my new passion and decided to join me in learning a martial art. There was a kung fu class which took place at the same location but on different nights, and this suited his schedule better than the karate class. I was happy that he was joining me in my new hobby, and had no problem jumping ship from one martial art to another. Kung fu also had the Bruce Lee association, which made it very appealing in my eyes. I was also excited about having an interest in common with my dad.

FOR MOST OF my childhood I only ever saw my father at weekends. During the week, he went from shop to shop all over Ireland, collecting orders for different types of hardware. He made good money doing this, but it meant that we didn't see much of him. He occasionally brought me with him when I was on school holidays and I got to see quite a bit of Ireland that way. We got to know each other better on these trips too, but I'd often get car sick and this made such trips difficult. I would always have to sit in the car and wait while he went into the shops because he didn't want me wandering around a strange place by myself, and I would end up spending much of these days alone. Nevertheless, I grew to love this time together, because my father would talk and talk, and tell me about his life. He was my father and I worshipped him, like I suspect most children worship their fathers.

On one of our trips, he gave an inspirational talk which affected me greatly. He told me about his hopes and fears, things he had never spoken of before. My father had left school at 12 years of age, but through pure determination and a refusal to give up, he had managed to carve out a career for himself. He was about to launch his own company, even though he could barely read. He was realising his dreams and he promised me that I could achieve any ambition if I was willing to put in the hard work and devote myself to my goal. I believed him.

He confided in me that he too had worshipped his own father, but his affection was never really returned. He had 12 other children to compete with for the attention of his hero. What's more, he also had to compete with alcohol. It was 'the drink' that was my grandfather's real love, and his large family came second in his list of priorities most of the time. They got close for a brief period before my grandfather died, when they spent a few weeks travelling around Ireland together. They learnt about each other's inner thoughts and feelings, but so many years had already been wasted and there was not much time left in the old man's life. I was determined that history would not repeat itself. My dad shared this determination and believed that we really had a special relationship. He often told me that we were more like brothers than father and son.

I WENT TO kung fu class four or five times a week. Dad went to classes with me at the weekends, and we practised together when he was at home. He wasn't able to devote that much time to kung fu so his progress was slow, but he enjoyed the classes all the same. He expressed his admiration for my progress and this made me feel proud of my efforts which spurred me on to improve even more. A famous saying in martial arts is that 'the person you need to beat is the person you were yesterday.' I practised every single day and steadily got better. My hard work was rewarded when after a year I was asked to teach the younger kids—or 'pee-wees'—as we called them.

Aside from the physical benefits, martial arts also introduced me to new ideas which helped fill a void in my life. These Eastern philosophies provided me with meaning and purpose; a system of thought that helped me deal with feelings I found unbearable at times. Kung fu philosophy provided a new way of looking at the world that made sense to me and this was something that I had been yearning for.

Previously, I had turned to Christianity for the answers to the big questions. I once attempted to read the bible from cover to cover, but instead of finding answers, it left me feeling confused and fearful. I couldn't achieve the same solace and certainty that others around me seemed to have in their religion. When I asked priests about religion they would answer that it was about faith. Many people who I both admired and respected were comfortable with Catholic teachings, but I had too many doubts. I was an altar boy and often said readings in mass, but I wasn't convinced about the whole thing. I wanted it all to be true, but my doubts were like an itch that I just couldn't stop scratching.

I can still remember the first time that I really thought about death, when I considered what it actually meant, and how one day, it would come for me too. These thoughts terrified me, and I lay awake for weeks thinking about them. For some reason I knew that adults couldn't give me any real answers so I just let the fears tumble around in my head. These fears got progressively worse as the years went by. I rebelled against the religion of my family and friends when I was 13, but this gave me no real comfort. I felt angry and let down by the church. It wasn't until years later that I realised Christianity wasn't the problem. It worked for millions of people; the problem was that it just didn't work for me.

Kung fu introduced me to Buddhism, Daoism, and more significantly for me, to meditation, as a means of developing the mind. I began to believe that there lay an escape from my fear of death in this outlet for my mind. I quickly developed an affinity with these ideas from the East because they answered many of the questions which had haunted my sleepless nights, and mirrored many of my own conclusions. I didn't see these philosophies as an alternative to Christianity, but as tools that anybody could use to make life easier to manage. These beliefs came into my life and made me feel more at peace with the world, at least for a while.

MY CLASS COMPETED in kung fu championships which took us to different parts of Ireland and to Birmingham in England once a year. I was always expected to do well in these events but I often felt like I had underperformed. I came second a few times, but usually fell apart on the day despite all my practice. I took solace in the fact that there was a lot more to martial arts than winning competitions. My goal was to become a professional martial artist, most likely an instructor, and if my life had taken a different path then maybe I would have achieved this ambition.

The main rival in my club was an older boy who often beat me in competitions. He was much more muscular than I was, and he always remained calm in the midst of a flurry of punches or kicks. I was praying for the day when he would be moved out of my age bracket so I would have more of a chance of winning. I believed his victories over me were unfair because he never seemed to train anywhere near as hard as I did. At this time I was going for a run in the mornings before school, and then I would practice kung fu for an hour after breakfast. After school I would train for at least another hour. All this was on top of my martial art classes. Even though I didn't always do as well as I would have liked in competition, I loved the intensive training. I couldn't imagine why anyone would want to live any other kind of life.

ALTHOUGH KUNG FU had taken over my imagination, my fascination with alcohol still remained. The older boys and men in the club drank and sometimes made fools of themselves. These crazy drinking sessions usually took place when we were on our way to competitions. Despite being underage, one of my friends from the class managed to get his hands on a bottle of vodka on one such trip, and almost drank himself into a coma. According to my other team-mates he had nearly choked on his own vomit. I missed out on all the action, however, because I was travelling separately with my father. When I saw my friend again I looked at him with a new sense of awe. His drinking had added a new dimension of character to him, at least in my eyes. Getting drunk and running amok seemed so exciting to me.

CHAPTER 5

DURING THE FOUR years that I trained in kung fu I made annual trips to England to fight in one of the main martial arts championships there. This trip was something that I looked forward to, and I intensified my training even further as the event neared. It was on one of these trips that my life was turned upside-down. My father confided in me that his relationship with my mother was in serious trouble, and that their marriage was on the verge of collapse. My parents were always fighting but I had no idea that things had gotten this bad between them. I was so devastated by my father's revelations that I couldn't go through with the competition, and demanded to be brought back home to Ireland.

At the time, I was incredibly angry and upset by the demise of my parents' relationship, and the only place I could vent my rage was on the punch bag. I knew that their relationship was over, and that it was just a matter of time before it became official. Words cannot explain how betrayed I felt by it all. I had always imagined that my parents would stay together, despite the fighting, and I was completely unprepared when their marriage finally ended. I probably never really got over it.

For a while I managed to hold things together by pumping all my anger into my martial arts practice. Meditation also helped me to ease the fury and sorrow spinning around inside my head. As time went on though, it all became too much. One night I decided to check if alcohol would help me to forget about my problems. I had seen adults let their hair down and forget all their worries when they were drunk, and I hoped it would help me to escape in the same way. I had been left baby-sitting my two sisters but they were asleep in bed so I decided to check out our drinks cabinet.

Our drinks collection consisted of a few spirits which were kept for special occasions like Christmas. Sometimes my mother would use the whiskey for making cakes, but otherwise, I can't remember either of my parents drinking from these bottles. They were reserved for guests.

On the night in question, I selected a bottle of Smirnoff Vodka and half-filled a tumbler with the clear liquid. I topped up the rest of the glass with orange juice. As this was my first time drinking spirits so I had no idea what to expect. I was a bit hesitant to take the first sip; I felt that by drinking the vodka I would be crossing a line between my life now and some new life but I decided to go with the unknown. I needed to escape the feelings of anger and frustration which felt like they might rip me apart.

I drank the first mouthful and almost threw it straight back up. It tasted disgusting, and I couldn't imagine anybody drinking it for pleasure. I had heard that vodka was tasteless so this came as quite a surprise to me. I didn't want to drink this vile stuff but decided, in the interest of experimentation, that I should at least see if I could get some type of buzz from it. My previous experience with alcohol had been so limited that I expected to feel something straight away.

I sipped the drink slowly, and by the time I reached the bottom of the glass, I was still not really feeling any effect. I topped up my tumbler again with half vodka and half orange juice. Realising that this amount of vodka would probably be noticed as missing from the bottle, I filled it up with water from the tap so my parents would be none the wiser.

The next glass went down more easily. It didn't taste so bad now, and I felt quite mature sitting watching the television, drinking my vodka and orange. I was even starting to feel something. I refilled my glass again, this time being careful to drink more slowly.

I hadn't drunk much from this glass when my head started to feel like it was swelling. I began to laugh hysterically at the television and knew what it felt like to be drunk. My head felt dizzy so I tested this by standing up. We had a sofa and two armchairs in the sitting room, and for a few minutes I amused myself by falling drunkenly from one to the other. This was great fun for a while, but then the nausea hit and it wasn't fun anymore. I got sick.

I fell up the stairs and into the bathroom where I spewed my guts up. I continued vomiting for a long time until all that was left were dry heaves. I rested my head against the cool toilet bowl and wanted to just drag myself into bed and sleep. Before I could do that, however, I knew I would have to clean up the mess downstairs, and add more water to the now three-quarters empty vodka bottle.

I dragged myself back down to the sitting room. The commotion had not woken either of my sisters, which was lucky as they were not very good at keeping secrets. I had to ease myself along the wall to make it down the stairs. I wanted to get sick again, but managed to hold it back. I eventually cleaned up the mess I had made downstairs and hid the evidence of my activity in the drinks cabinet. The sitting room smelled of vomit so I sprayed furniture polish everywhere. When I was satisfied that all evidence of my drunken antics had been destroyed, I crawled back up to my room.

The room was spinning around me as I lay in bed. I felt very sorry for myself. I worried that my parents might wonder why I wasn't up waiting for the bottle of Coke and packet of crisps they would bring me back from the pub. I prayed to God that they would leave me alone because there was no way I would be able to hide my drunken state. I promised the universe, and anyone who may have been listening, that I would never drink alcohol again. And I meant it. I could see that drinking was not a path I wanted to follow.

The next day my parents showed no signs of suspicion at my going to bed early. I suppose they both had enough on their minds and it wasn't too long after this incident that they went their separate ways. This had a calamitous effect on me.

My FATHER LEFT, and the atmosphere at home became unbearable. I never thought that he could just walk out on me or my family. He moved to Cork, and before long he was living with a new girlfriend. I had to stay at home with my mother who wasn't coping too well. My grandmother did what she could to keep the family together, but I just wanted to leave. I had begged my father to take me with him, but he'd refused. I told him that he couldn't just leave me, but he said he had no choice.

Instead, he sent me to live with his younger brothers and sisters who lived in his old home in Rathmichael. I was relieved with this proposal and couldn't wait to leave home. I adored my aunts and uncles, and a chance to actually live with them was a dream come true. However, it became clear a few days into the move that it wasn't going to work out. The responsibility of having to look after me began to cause friction in the house. My aunts and uncles were all young and single, with lives of their own, and it was too much to expect them to raise a teenager. Even though I understood this, I couldn't help feeling that all the adults in my life were abandoning me, so I reluctantly returned home.

I became more disruptive and troublesome, and spent a lot of time having screaming matches with my mother. My emotions were all over the place, and I started to feel like I was going crazy. I threw my stereo down the stairs on one occasion when I lost my temper. My grandmother did her best to help rein me in, but I was out of control. My mother already had a lot on her plate and I was only making things worse.

Eventually my behaviour became too much for her, and she agreed to let me go stay with my father. I was very excited about the move—I thought this could be a new start for me, a chance to escape the mess that my life had become. I would have a chance to reinvent myself with new friends in a new location. Too many bad memories had been created in Dublin recently, and I needed to get away from all of it.

I felt a mixture of guilt and relief on leaving home. Not only was I walking out on my mother, I was also abandoning my two sisters. I convinced myself that it would be better for them if I left. I loved my sisters, but I thought that I would go mad if I stayed at home. How would that help them? They were much younger than me, and at least they had each other. They also had a close relationship with our grandmother, but I felt close to nobody. I knew they were probably in a lot of pain too, but all I could think about was my own loss. I told myself that they were too young to really understand what was going on. I couldn't see past me.

THE MOVE TO Cork went well initially. I made a few friends, and coming from the capital city made me somewhat of a novelty. The cracks soon began to show however. Some of it was my father's fault, some of it was my own. I was 15 and out of control. I started getting into trouble. I fell in with a group who were involved in petty crime. We robbed cassette tapes from cars and altar wine from the church. We drank whatever alcohol we could lay our hands on before reaching the school gate in the morning, and then swayed through school assembly.

Naturally, my school worked suffered. I went from being in the top class in my previous school to the lowest one in this new school. I changed from doing the intermediate certificate, which I needed if I wanted to stay in school for the final three years, to doing a group certificate which seemed practically worthless. Nobody noticed my rapid academic decline, and it felt like the education system had given up on me just like everyone else had. I returned the sentiment and lost all interest in education.

The inevitable happened when I was expelled from the school at the end of the year for vandalism. The police got involved and they wanted to charge me with breaking into cars, as well as causing damage to the school. They agreed to drop the charges on the condition that I return to Dublin and make a statement which implicated my new friends; I was ashamed of myself for blabbing—I felt like a coward but in the end I was relieved to be going home to Dublin.

IT IS TEMPTING for me now to blame all my later woes on this period of my life, but that would be unfair. It would also be disingenuous. I know people who have suffered worse childhoods than mine, and they didn't end up as drunks or drug addicts. It is also tempting for me to imagine what would have happened if my school days hadn't been disrupted by the breakdown of my parent's marriage. Maybe I would have finished school and gone on to do great things at university. This could all be self-delusion though; I'm sure everyone sees themselves as a misunderstood genius at some point in their lives. I was a bright kid who may have done better if his life had been different, but maybe not.

CHAPTER 6

SELF-DELUSION IS a potent thing: you can convince yourself of almost anything. My school days were now over, and even though I knew it was mostly my own fault, I still felt it was unfair. All the same, leaving school brought me a sense of relief. School had been a burden prior to my parents' separation. After it, and with my plunging grades, education seemed pointless to me. My father had quit school at 12 years of age, and he seemed to be doing fine. Most of the adults around me were disapproving, however; they warned me that times had changed and now you needed 'the pieces of paper' if you wanted to get anywhere in life. Jobs were scarce in Ireland at the time but I managed to get a place on a youth training scheme called ANCO, and was optimistic about the future.

The ANCO course would not only prepare me for the world of work, it would also pay me for my troubles. Except for a brief part-time job and some baby-sitting here and there, this was to be my first wage packet. It wasn't a lot of money, but enough for me to feel like an independent adult.

Earning a wage meant, in my eyes anyway, that I was entitled to drink alcohol whenever I wanted. My mother nagged me about underage-drinking but came to accept that she was powerless to stop me. My father was also angry about my drinking, but he couldn't control me. As far as I was concerned, his views were immaterial now.

I had no qualms about breaking the underage drinking laws, which stipulated that it was illegal to sell alcohol to anyone under 18 years of age; the problem was that I looked my age. To circumvent the law I began hanging out with a bunch of lads from the ANCO course who had similar problems getting served in bars. At the weekends we would send the oldest looking member of our group to buy booze, and then drink our flagons of cider in various outdoor locations in south Dublin.

We could only afford to drink on the weekends but those nights were magical; everything was new and exciting. The restrictive Dublin of my school days now seemed full of possibilities. Growing up in south Dublin, I had taken its breathtaking scenery for granted; now, I was appreciating it with fresh eyes. A favourite drinking spot of ours was on top of Killiney Hill, where we would gaze down on Dublin bay. We'd laugh and joke and drink for hours. If we'd managed to get any girls to join us, we'd spend the night trying to impress them, outdoing each other in our drunken antics. Often, we'd stop just to admire the sight of the sea below which seemed connected to the night sky, and the lights sparkling from boats which looked like stars. I felt so connected to my friends, and to the world, in those moments.

I LIKED HOW booze made me feel, but my tolerance for it was low in the beginning. I didn't like the taste of cider, but it was the cheapest way for us to get drunk. After finishing a two-litre bottle I'd spend the next ten minutes vomiting it all back up, but the fun we had once the alcohol began to work its magic easily made up for the wretched spewing. I was in awe of my friends who were able to finish two flagons and still maintain a conversation. I felt like a bit of a lightweight because I couldn't drink as much as my friends, who teased me about my tolerance levels. This only made me even more determined to become an experienced, seasoned drinker.

Our little gang eventually discovered a nightclub where we could get served. On Sundays we'd make our way to a teenage-friendly bar in south Dublin and party our heads off. Our lack of funds meant that would still hit the cider before going anywhere; once inside the club we would only be able to afford a couple of pints and maybe a rum and blackcurrant juice. Going to a club and not getting as drunk as possible seemed absurd and pointless.

As good as the outdoor booze picnics had been, I felt like I had found heaven in proper drinking establishments. Just as I'd once given myself completely to kung fu, I now gave myself completely to alcohol. My future seemed bright again, and this path would not involve the hard work of becoming a professional martial artist, but instead would be so easy that even I couldn't fuck it up. I'd eventually get a full-time job; it didn't matter what job so long as it funded my partying and boozing. Work was a means to an end; a way to obtain 'beer tokens' as my drinking buddies referred to their wages. I would eventually meet a girl, we'd get married and have kids. I'd go to the bar everyday after work, and go out drinking with my wife at the weekends. A perfect life, or so I believed.

Alcohol offered far more than just a temporary reprieve from life's difficulties. It opened up a whole new world for me, and it introduced me to a new version of myself. A few drinks and I felt completely at ease with who I was for the first time. I could look people in the eye, and not feel embarrassed about myself. A few drinks and my past wasn't so important, and the future held no terror. Alcohol was a way to cheat life; a means to protect yourself from all the bumps.

Drinking also helped me to discover the wonderful world of women. It gave me the tools to feel more confident around them. I lost my virginity one night after a disco in Dalkey, a village in south Dublin. It wasn't exactly a moment of passion and romance, with my being too drunk and cold to enjoy it, and the girl later complaining that her knickers were full of leaves. The real pleasure though came afterwards; I had finally crossed the threshold from boyhood to manhood. I gave all my gratitude to alcohol—not many girls would agree to have sex in a damp cold field in the middle of the night if they were sober.

THE ANCO COURSE ended, and I got a job in a supermarket. Working at Dun Laoghaire Shopping Centre, which was located on the outskirts of Dublin, also provided me with a hectic social life. Over one hundred employees worked full-time at Quinnsworth, a supermarket in the Centre; most of them were going out with or married to other employees, and we all socialised together. I was still underage, but working in the shopping centre meant that I now had no trouble getting into bars. I no longer wasted my time with outdoor drinking and underage discos. The full-time job meant full-time wages; I no longer needed to drink cheap cider.

I was now earning proper money and had no trouble spending it. I would give a bit to my mother for housekeeping and the rest went on pints of Budweiser. I didn't save a penny, and I didn't go on holidays. I would start drinking on Friday night and would be borrowing money off my grandmother by Sunday. I lived from pay packet to pay packet, but that was fine by me; life was great and the future could take care of itself.

My tolerance for alcohol increased somewhat but I would still puke my guts up when I drank. The only difference was that I usually managed to last until the end of the night before vomiting. I suffered awful hangovers too, but my young body could handle the abuse, and a punishing hangover became something to boast about: 'Great night last night; feel shit today though.'

Sunday morning was my favourite time to be hungover, because I knew that it would only last until lunch time when the bars would open, and then I could start drinking again. I would go and sit with my grandfather in the pub. No longer was I left behind while the adults went for a few weekend beers; I had earned my place in the pub with them. My grandfather no longer cringed at my every word; alcohol had made me one of the lads and my penchant for saying the wrong thing became part of my charm.

Alcohol gave rhythm and purpose to my life; it made me feel good and like I belonged. To me, non-drinkers were the ones who had a problem; they were missing out on the real happiness in life. Only religious freaks and weirdos didn't drink as far as I was concerned. I littered my speech with one-liners about how living for the day was the important thing. These early days of drinking were so happy and simple. I didn't care about what the point of it all was anymore; I had no more existential angst. My purpose was to drink and have fun. So long as I had money to drink the world was a beautiful place, I didn't know that these feelings couldn't last.

ONE OF MY favourite things about drinking was that you never knew where you'd end up once you were on a good session. Things you'd never even consider doing when you were sober suddenly seemed like a great idea. I loved the spontaneity of it all. A few beers and caution went to the wind. We lived near a major port and would often hear stories of people getting drunk and waking up in Wales. Getting smashed seemed like a big adventure, where anything was possible.

I knew that alcohol also had harmful effects and wasn't exactly healthy, but I wasn't even 18 years old yet and I felt invincible. The idea that I could actually be doing myself serious harm seemed absurd to me. I was having too much fun to care anyway.

At this stage, all my heroes were big drinkers. I admired Brendan Behan, both for his skill as a writer and for his notoriety as a hardened drinker. He was the ultimate stereotypical drunken Irishman, who brought his typewriter to the pub. His reputation in Dublin was legendary, and I would listen in awe when my grandfather related tales he witnessed first hand of Behan's drunken antics. Behan died from alcohol abuse when he was just 41 years old, and seemed unrepentant for his lifestyle up until the end, but he reiterated to me the importance of living life at full-blast and to hell with the begrudgers! I didn't see his death as a lesson in alcoholism or wasted talent—instead I saw alcoholism as a sign of great artistic depth.

I also loved the Pogues and their mix of punk and folk music sounded like the soundtrack to my life. One of my favourite songs by them, *Streams of Whiskey*, was written about Behan. Many of the Pogues lyrics celebrated active alcoholism, which made them appealing to me. They encapsulated the spirit of punk and drunkenness.

Just as Bruce Lee had been my idol when kung fu was my passion, famous alcoholics took his place as alcohol became my new life's passion.

I MET A girl called *Hannah* who I thought might be the woman to fill the missing piece in my life; the wife who would have my dinner waiting when I came home from the pub. She had different ideas though. She only wanted someone to bring her to her debutante dance, the end of year celebration when we finished our final year of school. My plans for the future must have sounded fairly bleak compared to her own hopes after university. Once her dance was over, she dumped me.

At the time I was a young fool and her rejection devastated me so I hit the drink hard. One night I smashed a brick in my own face, in an attempt to feel the pain that was tearing me apart inside physically. I met some of her friends another night and made a total arse of myself, telling them how shit my life had become without *Hannah*. Outwardly, they were conciliatory, but I knew that they were thinking 'Get this lunatic away from me.'

The songs of Billy Bragg, the British singer-songwriter provided an outlet for my sorrow, and as the weeks went by, I forgot all about *Hannah*. I gravitated towards a group of older lads who were hard drinkers and big womanisers. They introduced me to the world of night-clubs. One in particular had a reputation and just drinking there gave me the status of being a bit of a lad. Most of this group lived in Sallynoggin so I began staying at my grandmother's at the weekend. *Miami Vice*, an American television series about two detectives, was all the rage on television and we would try to emulate its characters by wearing similar clothes with rolled-up sleeves. We'd walk home in the early hours singing sixties' songs. If we were feeling energetic we'd race each other through people's front gardens, jumping over fences, barging through bushes, screaming as loud as we could, and hoping to get chased by angry home owners. The next day I'd be covered in scratches and bruises. On really good nights, I would hook up with a woman, or end up at an all-night party.

My older friends shared their wisdom with regards to women. They told me how it was a numbers game and the most important asset was the ability to accept rejection and move on to the next target. They explained that in every bar or club there would always be a certain percentage of women who were willing to sleep with you—the trick was to find them.

They warned me of the dangers of getting involved in relationships because one-night-stands were where the real fun was. I was an eager student and found their methods did work, but quickly learned that one-night-stands weren't always so enjoyable, at least not afterwards when all the panting was over and you were left lying there feeling awkward. I didn't tell them this though because they would have seen me as a bit of a freak. I didn't even like to admit it to myself. I reasoned that one-night-stands were like my early attempts at alcohol and that I would soon develop a tolerance for them. It turned out that there was some truth in this.

As my 18th birthday was approaching, I developed a bit of wanderlust. I regularly accompanied friends, who were forced out of Ireland by unemployment and lack of opportunity, to the ferry port in Dun Laoghaire. They would return later with stories of how much better life was abroad. At the time, I was no longer satisfied with a future of working behind a check-out. I wanted something else, but I had no idea what. I sensed that whatever it was, I wouldn't find it in Dublin, or even Ireland. I wanted to travel the world and see all there was to be seen. I needed another fresh start, but this time there would be no running after my father. I was going on this journey alone.

CHAPTER 7

I FELL IN love with the English town of Oxford straight away. The mixture of yellow-stone historical buildings and young students gave the city a unique feel. As I explored my new home that first day it seemed that merely turning a corner could take me to another world. A side-alley off a modern street would lead to university buildings that belonged to a different age. The thing that amazed me the most was seeing 'Staff Wanted' signs outside so many shops and bars. Employment had been so scarce in Dublin that having my pick of jobs impressed me no end.

The help of a family friend meant that I had a job already waiting for me when I arrived in the city, however. The Westgate was a busy city centre bar that mostly catered for local business people during the day, and young pleasure-seekers at night. At weekends customers would queue up just for the privilege of drinking there. The Westgate didn't look much from the outside. In fact, it compared badly with the picturesque pubs normally associated with Oxford.

The attraction lay inside the doors. All the bar staff were under 30 years of age, most of us under 20, and we were all keyed up for having a good time. The Westgate had a reputation for being a happening place with friendly bar staff.

We had lots of fun behind the bar and partied along with the customers. The staff were allowed to have a beer if a customer bought us one, but we could only drink half pints as we needed to be sober enough to do our job. Most nights I had far more drinks bought for me than I could possibly consume. I was being paid to drink, and could hardly believe my luck.

Prior to arriving in England I worried that my Irish nationality would work against me. The Provisional IRA was frequently planting bombs there, and I suspected that the English blamed all Irish people for the activities of those few. I was pleasantly surprised, however, to find that my nationality was never an issue, and made life easier for me if anything. Many female customers said they liked my accent, and most of the English people I met had some Irish relatives. Sometimes people would make comments about the drunken Irish, but at the time I didn't see this as a criticism.

It was the late 80s, and there was plenty of money changing hands. One crowd of local businessmen would spend their lunch break standing at the bar, ordering bottle after bottle of champagne. They were friendly and would encourage us to join them if we weren't working that day; our different position on the economic food chain was irrelevant to them. One of them owned a travel agency and he always made sure the Westgate staff received cheap flight tickets. In return we made sure that they received good service and would compete for the right to serve their drinks. They would buy a bottle of champagne for £25 and they would usually give us £30 for it and tell us to keep the change. This was almost enough money to get drunk on so we were happy to get it.

The bar closed in the afternoons, and we would make up music tapes to pump out to the customers at night during this break. We all had different music tastes, and I would compete with the others to create tapes that would go down well in the bar. The biggest compliment was to have your tape played from beginning to end. When I first arrived in Oxford my music selection revolved around punk and Billy Bragg; this wasn't popular with the fun-lovers of Oxford. After a few weeks though, the city's optimistic mood worked its magic on me, and I developed a taste for more cheerful tunes. Before leaving Ireland I would have balked at the idea of listening to dance music, but now it was all I listened to.

It wasn't just my taste in music that was changing, I also began taking better care of my appearance. Many of my new friends were obsessive in their attempts to dress well, and far more of our conversations revolved around fashion than I previously would have expected among a group of guys. The clothes I arrived with were bought on the basis of affordability, but my friends thought that this was a fool's attitude. They warned me that my ability to attract women would be seriously limited if more of an effort wasn't made on my part. The old clothes went in the bin, and I began building a new collection of more expensive garments.

My new friends tried to improve their chances with the opposite sex by maintaining a year-long tan. The family friend who had arranged the job for me kept a sunbed above the bar, and we all fought to have as much access to this as possible. The tan and new clothes did a lot to boost my confidence, and this in turn increased my chances with women.

I arrived in Oxford at the beginning of summer when the city was revelling in the sun. The days were hotter than what I was used to in Ireland. There were beer gardens everywhere; the ideal place to while away balmy afternoons and early evenings. It was paradise. I loved to spend my free time at a bar called the Head of the River, where I could sit and get pleasantly drowsy beside the busy Oxford waterway. Life felt aglow with hope and happiness on those precious days.

JUST AS IT had been in Dublin, Sunday was my favourite day in Oxford. I usually arranged to have this day off from work. I'd always wake up hung-over from the previous night, and would take Sunday mornings slowly. I lived in staff accommodation above the Westgate, and would make my way down to the bar when it opened at noon. Sometimes I would just stay there drinking happily all afternoon. It never seemed odd to be spending my day off drinking where I worked—all the staff did this. It was a cheap session because customers would make sure that I always had a free pint of lager in front of me. Other Sundays, I would be more adventurous and hit the Brew House Bar down the road. Sunday afternoon was for nursing a beer slowly as it gently eased the effects of the previous night's drinking.

My hangover would be completely cured by the time afternoon bar closing arrived but I'd always be in the mood to continue drinking. Because the pubs closed for a longer period on Sundays, bar staff from all over the city had an opportunity to get together. We'd have wine picnics down by the river or play drunken football matches against rival bars and the winners would receive a case of beer. I enjoyed all these activities so long as there was alcohol involved. When Sunday evening arrived the pubs would be open again and a group of us would drift from bar to bar until we had our fill. If our appetites were not sated by last orders we would hit a nightclub.

In almost two years working at the Westgate I never once went to bed sober. I would drink all day at work, and I'd continue drinking until well after the bars had closed. I didn't think my behaviour was at all strange; this is what everyone else seemed to be doing around me. Occasionally people would make comments about my excessive drinking habits, albeit usually in a light-hearted way. The sad fact is that I enjoyed the reputation of being the stereotypical drunken Irishman. I loved it when people mentioned my drinking exploits, although I felt a little uneasy when I couldn't remember what had happened myself. Still, this was all part of the fun for me. As I would frequently say: 'It must have been a good night last night, because I can't remember a fucking thing about it.' Apparently I even split up with a girlfriend during one of these blackouts, and I had no idea the next day why she seemed a bit off with me.

When people occasionally made more serious comments about my drinking, I would be full of indignation. How dare anyone question me? There was no way I was going to apologise for trying to enjoy my life. I was always suspicious of these begrudgers, and thought that they had some hidden agenda. As far as I was concerned they needed to let their hair down and leave hedonists like me alone.

But more and more frequently, I started messing up while drunk. I'd insult somebody or do something else equally stupid. I'd be bashfully apologetic the next day, and admit that maybe I needed to slow down a bit. I was willing to concede that I did indeed drink too fast, but, then again, this just seemed to be a part of my personality as I also spoke and ate fast too. I would make vague promises to change in the future, but I had no intention of following through by making any adjustments to my drinking habits. If anything, I would have liked to have drunk more. Just like headaches and vomit, saying sorry became another unfortunate side effect of the drinking life—side effects that I was more than willing to tolerate.

I WAS GIVEN the responsibility of taking care of the cellar in the Westgate. With this came even more opportunities to drink. When a barrel needed changing I would be able to escape down to the cellar and knock back a bottle of strong Pils lager. I enjoyed such sneaky drinks even more than the half-glass waiting for me behind the bar because it felt like I was bending the rules a little.

The best part of taking care of the cellar was the pipe cleaning. I tended to do it early on a weekday morning. There were over 20 pipes which would need to be sanitised by passing a cleaning solution through them, followed by water to rinse them out. After each pipe was cleaned, the task of tasting the beer or lager to make sure that no trace of cleaning fluid remained, fell to me. I presume the usual protocol is to taste the alcohol and then spit it out, but I preferred to pour myself a half pint each time and drink most of it. By the time I got through all the pipes I would be swaying.

The sad truth is that I loved being inebriated while pretending to be sober. It gave me a great feeling of getting away with something, of cheating the system and winning. Who would want to live life with all its humdrum problems when you could feel chilled out and happy all the time? Nothing mattered after a few beers, it was all just a show. Even death, my greatest childhood fear, could be looked upon with amusement when I had consumed alcohol.

CHAPTER 8

I HAD BEEN working at the Westgate for over a year when *Sarah* came into my life. She had been working as a nanny in Germany before she came to work in the bar part-time while waiting for something better to turn up. *Sarah* had bright ginger hair which she kept in an unruly punk style and wore army surplus clothes. I thought she was nice when she arrived in the Westgate, but didn't give her any further consideration. It wasn't until she rejected my advances during a staff night out that I developed any sort of romantic interest in her, and at that, it wasn't exactly very romantic.

I had a theory about women which was based on the notion that the more you had, the more you got. This theory originated from my Dublin drinking buddies and it reflected my own personal experiences. If you hit a dry patch with women it was very hard to escape because, conversely, the less you had, the less you got. I theorised that women instinctively knew when men were in demand, and they were attracted to this. Before meeting *Sarah*, I had been having a particularly fruitful period with women, and I worried that her rejection might signal the beginning of a dry patch. I decided that I needed to salvage something by getting *Sarah* to change her mind about me.

So I launched a campaign aimed at getting her into bed. I complimented her all the time and asked her out at least once a day. After a few weeks she relented. Her agreeing to go on a date was actually a misunderstanding. A workmate mentioned to *Sarah* that I was hitting the booze particularly hard recently because of her continued rejection. Of course he was joking: I was getting drunk because I liked getting drunk. So *Sarah* decided to go on a date with me out of pity, and I was happy enough to go along with this. Not too long after that, we became a couple.

Sarah and I spent a lot of time together, which meant I had less time for drinking with my Oxford friends. The only problem with this lifestyle was that *Sarah* wasn't much of a drinker, and I had no intention of reducing my intake. When we were both off work on Sundays, we would go for long walks in the Oxfordshire countryside; *Sarah* would enjoy the country air, and I would be in search of the ideal village pub. We'd walk until early evening when the bars would open, and then we'd end up in a quaint rural inn. I would settle down to a night of drinking, my enjoyment just being disrupted by my constantly having to persuade *Sarah* to stay for 'just one more drink'. When she wasn't complaining to me about my drinking habits, *Sarah* was great company. By that, I mean she was willing to sit there and listen while I'd go on long-winded rants about everything and anything.

She didn't feel the same way about Oxford as I did, however, and she wasn't there long before she got itchy feet. She also thought I drank too much because there was too much temptation in Oxford. She talked about her life in Germany, and this rekindled my desire to see the world. At first, I felt hesitant about leaving a job and lifestyle that suited me, but the desire to travel, and the fear of losing *Sarah*, motivated me to go for it. We decided that our first stop should be Dublin so that *Sarah* could see Ireland, and maybe we could earn some money to go travelling abroad. *Sarah* realised that I wouldn't save a penny living in Oxford, and I didn't make my doubts about my prospects for saving back in Dublin known.

WE STAYED WITH my mother and sister in Dublin for a few weeks, until an uncle organised a room above his business partner's shop for us. He was kind enough to arrange a job for me in the shop also. The accommodation was right in the heart of the city, and it provided a whole new world of pubs for me to explore. *Sarah's* hope that moving out of Oxford might reduce my drinking turned out to be wildly optimistic, as I began drinking even more. In the beginning I rationalised this by saying that I needed to catch up with old friends, but as the weeks passed by, it was evident that this was just an excuse, and she became less understanding.

My descent into addiction, or full blown alcoholism, quickened and to *Sarah*'s horror a new and alarming element entered my life: the early house. I had first visited this establishment a couple of years previously when I had accompanied my then girlfriend to her end of school dance. After partying all night in the city, we went to the early house at 7am when it opened. These bars catered for night workers, but I thought it was the greatest idea ever and the memory had stayed with me. Now that I was back in Dublin, and living in the city, I had the perfect opportunity to check out the early house.

I only worked in my uncle's shop a few days a week so I had plenty of time off. *Sarah* was now working in a crèche and she was out during the day. On my days off I would walk her to the train station at 7am, and as soon as she was out of sight, I'd hit the bars. I made the mistake of telling her about the first time I went to the early house after leaving her at the train; *Sarah*'s reaction was enough to stop me ever telling her again. My silence didn't do much to ease her mind, however. She became more vocal in her disapproval at coming home from work to find me sozzled every evening.

All this drinking meant that our finances were in a dire state. On one of our lowest evenings, after I'd once again drank all the money we had, we resorted to eating muesli with mayonnaise for dinner. As we didn't have enough money for milk, we thought mayo could be a good substitute—how wrong we were.

THE WORSE OUR finances became, the more desperate I became for alcohol. Getting drink was all I thought about. I lived in fear of the day when there would be no more money for booze. Even at this point, when I wasn't having fun anymore, and was drinking solidly every day just to cope with life's pressures, I didn't see myself as being dependent on alcohol. It was just the natural response to a downturn in luck. I couldn't see the hole I was digging for myself, or how my behaviour was ruining my future. Coming back to Dublin had clearly been a mistake. To handle this disappointment, I drank a lot, which in turn meant I had no money to leave Dublin. I was confident, though, that if *Sarah* remained patient then we would be on the move again soon. What I didn't realise was that it didn't matter where I was—it could've been Dublin, or London, or a paradise island in the Pacific—I still would have been drinking myself into oblivion, because I was already addicted to alcohol, I just couldn't see it.

At one point I sold *Sarah*'s cassette tapes out of desperation. She loved music and her treasured collection gave her a lot of joy, but all they represented to me on that day was their exchange value. I needed to drink and that was that. When she realised what I had done she lost it. As far as she was concerned, that was the last straw: we were over. I begged and pleaded and promised to change. Eventually, she gave me an ultimatum: we either left Dublin or we were definitely over.

OVER THE NEXT few weeks we managed to save enough money to go to her family home in Scotland. It was coming up to New Year's Eve, and I assured her that 1990 would see a reformed Paul. I had lied to her so often that I began to believe my own lies. But it wasn't to be—all that changed were the drinking venues. We may have been away from all the problems we'd had in Dublin, but a change in location wasn't the solution to those problems. Being in a different country was not much help to an alcoholic when there were as many opportunities to drink as there had been everywhere else. My drinking problem ran deeper than the location I was in.

We moved into a shared house, and *Sarah* was not amused to find that our housemate was an unemployed poet who liked to spend the day drinking cheap whisky. Needless to say we bonded immediately. I had always harboured a desire to become a writer but rarely finished my writing projects and never had the guts to show my work to anybody else. My new friend impressed me because he was living the writer's life and had no qualms about sharing his work. Officially, he made a living through social security payments, but he was a writer nonetheless. I'd spend hours listening attentively to his poetry as we worked our way through his daily supply of whisky. I got a job in a nightclub where my shift started in the evening, but as the days went by, it became harder and harder to leave the poetry sessions. I stopped going to work and blamed it on the bad influence that my new friend was having on me. *Sarah* decided that we needed to move again.

We moved to Glasgow and stayed with one of *Sarah*'s old school friends. I quickly found another job working in a bar. It was three months into the New Year when *Sarah* realised that I wasn't going to change. She'd had enough and decided to kick me out. This time, no amount of begging and pleading could change her mind. I decided to call her bluff and threatened to go back to Ireland. It backfired, however, when she said she thought it would be a good idea. I was devastated but also furious. She knew I didn't even have enough money to pay the bus fare into the city, and that the last place I wanted to go was back to Dublin. She gave me what money she had in her purse and wished me all the best so I took the £5, protesting that it wasn't enough to even get me out of Glasgow. She commiserated, but made it clear that this was no longer her problem. She wanted me gone. I left, believing that she would regret her decision once she thought I was really gone for good. I convinced myself she was just trying to give me a fright.

I spent most of the £5 in a local bar while giving *Sarah* time to change her mind. I still felt uncomfortably sober when I ran out of money for another pint. I rang her and was astonished to find that, instead of being relieved to hear from me, she was livid because I hadn't left the city. She guessed what had happened to the money she gave me. I managed to hitch my way to Stranraer Port where the ferry for Ireland departed; I arrived hoping that maybe a truck would be able to sneak me onto a boat. One of the drivers soon burst my bubble by telling me the trucks were checked prior to boarding.

Feeling utterly defeated, I took a big gulp, swallowed my pride, and rang my father. I expected him to be sympathetic and to help me out of my predicament but he asked if alcohol was part of the problem and I reluctantly admitted that it was. He arranged to pay for my boat fare and train ticket home but, needless to say, I didn't quite get the kind of sympathy I was after.

CHAPTER 9

I HAD THOUGHT that by admitting I had a problem with alcohol, my father would take control and sort my life out for me, but I discovered he was almost as helpless as I was to do anything. I went to stay with him in Cork for a few days, but all he could suggest was that I go to Alcoholics Anonymous (AA) meetings. I gave them a try, but didn't understand how these overly-earnest, smiley-happy old people could help me.

In truth, I didn't believe that alcohol was the problem. In my eyes the real issue was that people kept interfering with my desire to enjoy life. I didn't have a problem with drink; other people had a problem with my drinking. I convinced myself that people like *Sarah* had hang-ups about living life to the full, and because of their hang-ups, I was suffering. It seemed so unfair—excessive drinking was hardly unusual behaviour for a 20-year-old. The real problem, from my point of view, was that these busybodies could not be ignored. They had the power to make my life difficult or to withhold things which were important to me. I came to the conclusion that it was vital for me to learn to hide the worst excesses of my addiction. Giving it up, or even just cutting back a little, was never an option. That would have been ludicrous.

I viewed all this as a failure on my father's part to help me, and this period marked a low point in our relationship. Throughout the years up until this point I had continued to hero-worship him. I defended all his actions and really believed that he would do anything for me. I now saw that he was just as flawed as the rest of us. He had helped me to get back to Ireland, but once there he gave me the impression that I was being a burden; he had made a new life for himself and didn't want me messing things up for him. I suppose the other reason for his ineffectiveness was fear. He had already had to deal with an alcoholic father and now history was repeating itself.

I TRIED TO convince myself that *Sarah* would have me back; she just needed space to calm down. Our time apart would give me a chance to smarten up a bit, and at the very least learn to reduce the amount that I drank in public. I went back to Dublin and signed on for unemployment benefit; I now felt like a complete failure. This time apart from *Sarah* had made me realise just how important she had become to me. While travelling around Dublin I would often end up in places where we had once been together. Various things would remind me of her, and I'd have to hold back tears each time I thought of her. Finding a way to get back together with *Sarah* became the most important thing in my life, or at least that's what I told myself.

THE ONLY REAL friend that I had during this bleak period was alcohol. My former drinking buddies had all moved on with their lives but I used to seek out the company of others who, like me, wanted to do nothing but drink. This helped to erase *Sarah* from my memory and my lack of funds was the only thing holding me back. I struggled from one unemployment payment to the next and I borrowed where I could. Now I could only afford to drink in bars on dole day. The rest of the time drinking cheap cans of lager kept me going. I drank with anyone I could find and went outdoors with the underage drinkers and the long term unemployed.

I received my social welfare money every two weeks on a Wednesday. I would always ensure to be at the dole office a few minutes before bar opening time. As soon as I received the payment I would hit the bars around Dun Laoghaire and drink until closing time, rarely remembering how I got home the next day. Apparently, one night I almost choked on my own vomit. My family became more and more concerned about my lifestyle, and one morning I felt so ill and remorseful that I finally agreed to get help.

I went to my local GP who sent me to an addiction specialist. I tried to play down the extent of my drinking, but he decided that attendance at a treatment centre would be needed. The specialist put me on a drug called abstem, which would make me feel ill if I consumed alcohol. I went along with all this, but remained convinced that my problem had little to do with addiction. My main motivation in getting treatment was so I could win back *Sarah*, who had long since moved on.

The treatment centre was run by St John of Gods, which mortified me because in Ireland this name had always been associated with the mentally ill. If you heard that someone had spent time in St John of Gods you knew that it would be best to keep out of their way. I dreaded the prospect of being labelled as someone suffering from a mental illness, but I also felt very ashamed. I was angry for allowing myself to be talked into doing something which could ruin my reputation. But I also felt trapped into going along with things. I wasn't sure about my rights and I worried that if I had a change of heart and decided to quit treatment, I could possibly be forced to attend.

I went to the centre five days a week for three months. It was expected that I spend most of the day there but I was allowed to go home in the evenings. As well as the drunks and druggies, it also catered for people with mental health problems such as schizophrenia and manic depression. This only confirmed my suspicion that I was being treated like some sort of mentally unstable person, instead of someone who just drank a bit too much.

The nurse-in-charge made sure that I swallowed my abstem tablet each morning; this involved shuffling along in a queue with the other patients towards a plain-clothes nurse. As time passed, I began to see myself as a patient—the only thing missing was the pyjamas. The nurses explained, however, that we weren't referred to as 'patients' but 'clients'; I personally didn't understand the difference.

I was surprised on the first day to find out that they would be checking my liver function. To me this was absurd; I had never even considered the possibility that I could have damaged my liver. Cirrhosis was for the old homeless drunks who wore smelly coats and drank industrial spirits. As far as I was concerned, I only drank beer, so surely my vital organs were safe. The nurses soon paid truth to this, however. They told me that plenty of people in their twenties had damaged their livers beyond repair. It took over a week to get the results back from the liver test, and I worried the entire time. When the news did come back the nurses forgot to tell me, and it was only when I confronted them that they gave me the good news—my liver was safe, for the time-being at least.

The day at the centre consisted of attending group therapy, life-skills classes, and stress reduction sessions. I was also expected to go to AA meetings, but I tried to avoid these as much as possible. I tended to stay away from the other drunks in the centre because they all seemed old and grumpy. I found the druggies and depressives to be far more glamorous and would spend my time with them.

To my dismay, it wasn't possible to completely avoid AA. The philosophy of the day-centre was that alcoholics needed to attend meetings in order to stay sober. The message was constantly being drummed in that AA was the only solution, and without it there was no hope for people like me, but I wasn't convinced. I reluctantly joined the 12 step programme, or the 12 steppers as it's sometimes called, but I never opened my mouth. Sometimes the life stories told at the meetings were interesting, but mostly I just felt like I was wasting my time.

On a personal level, I hated the way the AA members would talk to me as if they could see right through me. I realise now that they could, but at the time the smiling earnest faces and the constantly repeated mantras like 'it works if you work it' and 'let go; let God' gave me the feeling of being in a cult. The dire predictions the AA old-timers made about what would happen if I drank again irritated me more than they scared me. Some of these people were sober over 20 years and still talked about how it was 'one day at a time'. As far as I was concerned, that sounded like a ridiculous way to live. I didn't want to spend the rest of my life missing alcohol.

After a few weeks of sobriety my mind cleared, and I began to appreciate the benefits of not drinking. I felt physically well and realised that for the last few years my body had felt ill most of the time. As I neared the

three month mark my health continued to improve
both physically and mentally. My motivation and
energy levels increased. I could see that my life teemed
with possibilities and a lot could be achieved while not
drinking.

While getting a haircut one day, the barber told
me about his own struggles with alcohol. He was my
age when he had been a drunk, but somehow he had
managed to get off it. He stayed sober for a year and
never had a problem with alcohol after that. He was
now a social drinker and was able to enjoy a few drinks
without over doing it. This gave me great consolation
and I decided I would try to stay sober for a few years
to give me time to become successful and make a bit of
money. Then, I figured, it would be possible for me to
safely enjoy a few beers now and again. I felt relieved
at this solution and it put my mind at ease.

ALTHOUGH I DIDN'T know it at the time, there was a
void in my life, which I believed was caused by *Sarah*'s
absence. I felt lost so I decided to get in touch with her
again. We decided that phone calls were too expensive
but we agreed to exchange letters at least once a week. I
was still desperate to get back with her, but she insisted
that we could only be friends. She claimed to be proud
of me for sorting out my drink problem, and this really
encouraged me. Eventually, she agreed to let me come
back to Scotland and stay with her until I found a job.

This was great news, because I just couldn't see a future for myself in Dublin.

I completed my time with St John of Gods and felt positive about the future. I stopped taking abstem but worried that without this deterrent I would go straight back on the booze. Thankfully I didn't and I managed to stay sober. The fact that I hadn't been drinking meant I'd saved a lot of money, and I used this to return to Scotland.

During our time apart *Sarah* had also gone through some major life changes. She had found religion and was now a Jehovah's Witness. This news caught me off guard. She had dropped hints in her letters about going to bible meetings, but I never paid much attention. Her new beliefs were now the main focus of her life, and she made it clear that if I got in the way of them she would have nothing to do with me anymore. While I had been back in Ireland *Sarah* had managed to get her own little flat. She allowed me to stay on her couch for a few days, but she was keen to get me into my own place. I wondered if this meant our love affair was over.

I WAS ADVISED by the addiction counsellors to avoid working in bars again, even though this severely reduced my employment options. I eventually found a job as a security guard but the wage was far less than a social security cheque so I gave it up after a few weeks. Employment opportunities in Glasgow were almost as bad as in Dublin, and it began to look as if a return to Ireland was the only option. Then the Westgate offered me my old job back, and I decided to go against the counsellors' advice.

Despite *Sarah*'s religious conversion, my desire for us to get back together remained. Her interest in the Jehovah's Witnesses had taken me by surprise, but I convinced myself that it was just a strange phase she was going through, and that she would later look back upon this time with embarrassment. I saw the move to Oxford as a temporary solution which would allow me to save a bit of money before once again facing the Glasgow job market. *Sarah* was sceptical about my ability to stay sober when surrounded by old temptations, but I was feeling confident; the plan to return to Glasgow and to *Sarah* was to be my priority and alcohol would not be permitted to get in the way. That was my resolute belief.

I HAD ONLY been away from Oxford for a year but a lot had changed in that time. Many of the old staff had left, and the mood in the bar seemed different somehow; not bad, just different. Initially I missed the way things had been, but within a few weeks the new bar staff felt like old friends, and it was like I had never left. Occasionally people would make comments about my previous drunken exploits, and I liked this but tried to always make it clear that those days were well behind me.

It turned out *Sarah* had been right to be sceptical about my ability to resist old temptations. Not long after returning to Oxford, I started drinking again, but unlike the dire predictions made by those in AA, I did seem to have more control, or at least that's what I thought. I came to believe that there had never been a problem in the first place, and that the experts were just scaremongers who made a living by making people feel guilty about enjoying themselves. I convinced myself they had brainwashed me into feeling uncomfortable around something which had given me so much pleasure in the past. I doubted that drinking would ever bring me quite as much joy as it had previously, but I decided to allow myself the occasional pint anyway.

Suddenly, living in Oxford became fun again, but I couldn't get *Sarah* and Scotland out of my head. I remained in constant contact with her and began travelling up to Glasgow every chance I got. These trips weren't easy due to the fact that I only had one full day off a week. I would take the night bus to Glasgow, and after spending the day with *Sarah* I would make the 12 hour journey back to Oxford for my afternoon shift. The people around me thought that my dedication to *Sarah* was either very impressive, or a bit fanatical. It was both.

On my visits to Glasgow to see *Sarah*, I managed to pick up work in another bar so I decided to return permanently. I slept on *Sarah*'s couch again for a few days before finding a room to rent. Her resistance to us becoming a couple again began to fade. She had been impressed by the effort I had made to spend time with her while back in Oxford. The only thing now separating us was her religion. She made it clear that there would be no sex before marriage, and she only wanted to marry someone who shared her passion for Jehovah. She tried to get me interested, and I even read some of the literature, but I had walked away from Christianity years before and had no desire to go back to it.

I WOKE UP one morning soon after my return to Scotland and realised two things. The first was that I no longer loved *Sarah*. I had gone to bed the night before, still thinking about how we could get back together, and woke up the next day with this longing completely dissipated. My other realisation was that I wanted to get drunk. I wanted to get pissed out of my head. I was fed up with holding myself back and walking away after only a couple of beers. I had just turned 21 and hadn't even had a party because I was afraid of what *Sarah* would say; she no longer celebrated birthdays and didn't know that I had been back drinking alcohol again. I felt as though life was passing me by and I decided that I needed to start having some fun again. I got cracking on my new plan straight away by hitting the bars as soon as they opened for the day. I never saw *Sarah* again.

CHAPTER 10

I STAYED IN Glasgow for a year and worked in a trendy city centre pub where I made a few friends. The management were nice to you so long as you did your work. I soon left, however, because they didn't allow me to drink behind the bar. I accepted a large cut in wages to go and work in a run-down pub in a rough area of the city. They didn't care if I drank behind the bar, and that was its only attraction for me.

The bar was situated across the road from a Salvation Army hostel, and most of our customers were homeless. This bar was a particular favourite with people down on their luck because the management allowed any leftover drink to be sold at a reasonable price. Part of my job was to pour any unfinished drinks into a large steel bucket kept behind the bar. This bucket of slops could contain any variety of booze, and few customers could still hold a conversation after a couple of pints of the stuff.

The great thing about the bar was that my drinking habits seemed tame compared to those around me;

there was no pretence of social drinking with this crowd. Our biggest seller was Super Lager, the strongest lager you could buy. Merely asking for it in some pubs was enough to get you kicked out. You could shit your pants or go for a piss in the middle of my new place of work and none of the other customers would raise an eyebrow. Drink had ruined these people and I swore that I would never allow myself to end up like them. I had no problem drinking with the customers in the bar if they were buying, but secretly I looked down my nose at them.

It was the Year of Culture in Glasgow, but most of the cultural festivities passed me by—I had no interest in anything that didn't involve alcohol. I lived in a cheap bed-sit which I never cleaned. I only went there to sleep. I spent a lot of the time feeling miserable and blaming my depression on the greyness of the city—it was so much easier to blame my surroundings than to consider that the problem might actually stem from me. I decided I needed a change of scenery. There was nothing keeping me in Scotland. A year earlier I had been desperate to move to Glasgow, but now I was even more desperate to leave it.

During my time at the treatment centre in Dublin we had a talk on the typical behaviours of an addict. One of these behaviours was called the 'geographical'— this is when the drunk or drug addict moves on to a new place every time they mess up in the hope that moving will make things better. Despite knowing of this tendency I didn't associate it with my own behaviour, and felt certain that a change of scenery would fix me.

Years later I heard a Thai monk relating a story to illustrate this inclination of drug addicts to move from place to place. In Thai Buddhist temples there are many stray dogs which are left there by owners who no longer want to take care of them. It is against the Buddhist precepts to kill animals so the monks end up having to look after these strays. You will often see dogs in the temples who are suffering from flea infestations. If you observe these dogs they will spend their day scratching, then moving to a new part of the temple, and then scratching again. They move around hoping to escape the fleas, not realising that they are carrying the fleas around with them.

This sums up the 'geographical' aspect to my personality perfectly; moving from place to place to escape the madness without realising that the madness was inside my own head.

I LEFT SCOTLAND. I went back to London, and found work in yet another public house. This new pub was off the Tottenham Court Road and mostly catered for students and professors from the University of London. After the slop-house in Glasgow it all seemed very high-class and luxurious. Customers here always made it to the toilet, and if people were too drunk to stand they would be asked to leave the premises.

Being surrounded by academics every day acted as a constant reminder of my own lack of qualifications. In Oxford I dealt with these feelings of inferiority through reverse-snobbery; I'd console myself by saying that these students had no common sense. I frequently quoted that hackneyed cliché that I went to the 'University of Life'. It was harder to bury these feelings now, however, and I was resentful that others seemed to have been given all the breaks while my options in life were so limited. I would overhear discussions in the bar about economics or social theory which made me feel like a bit of a dunce. I yearned to be part of the world of ideas but didn't think that it would ever be possible.

I HAD BEEN in London for a few months when I met *Lucy* during the course of one of my solo pub crawls on a day off work. On these all-day drinking sessions, I would always be on a quest to find the perfect bar—a place frequented by the perfect clientele and staff who would all welcome me like an old friend. My new best buddies would love me unconditionally and see the great potential that lay untapped inside me. They would fix me and put me on the road to success. In time I learned that this was the root of my problem. I never considered looking for these answers within myself, always expecting someone else to save me. A part of me really believed that such a place did exist and it was only a matter of time before I found it.

Most people would never drink alone, but for me, this was the best type of drinking. I loved drinking by myself: I'd allow the alcohol to free my imagination, and I'd lose myself in my own thoughts. I'd concoct plans in my mind and for a few hours my life would be full of possibility and hope for the future. The next day, I'd wake up thinking that these ideas were completely insane. I'd look forward to the time when I could do it all over again, and be drunk enough to dream up more possible scenarios for the future, maybe hitting on a winner eventually.

On the day I first encountered *Lucy*, I had been drinking in Camden Town, which was my favourite area of London because of its connection with the Indie music scene. It was an exciting place dedicated to young people who were up for a good time. Even while drinking alone it was possible to feel part of something trendy in Camden.

I frequently amazed myself with the amount of lager I could consume during these long drinking days; over 15 pints was the average, but sometimes I'd consume close to 20. I wouldn't drink fast, just tick along, always thinking about where to go for my next pint. Sometimes I felt like I could drink forever when I hit this mode. I never felt like I was getting any drunker, just happily numb.

Lucy worked in the last bar I hit that day. I thought she was attractive straight away, but didn't think that I had much of a chance with her, she seemed a bit out of my league. The day's worth of alcohol had made me chatty, and to my surprise, she actually seemed interested in what I was saying. She didn't just try and humour me with the intention of removing herself from the conversation at the first opportunity. She had customers to serve, but she kept on coming back to me and continuing our conversation. It didn't seem to bother her that I was half-hanging off the seat, or that I was struggling not to spill my drink.

I learned that *Lucy* was studying chiropody in university and only worked at the bar part-time to earn extra money because her family wasn't able to pay all her expenses. She came from Liverpool, and seemed down-to-earth and easygoing. Her laugh was loud and contagious and her mousy curly hair complemented her cute small nose and slight freckles perfectly.

I often returned to the bar in order to try and meet her and, eventually, I plucked up enough courage to ask her out on a date. To my amazement she said yes. We arranged to go to a nearby bar the following night. I left her at closing time and walked out into the London night feeling like a hormonal teenager again. The prospects of going on a date with this attractive, pleasantly laidback young lady left me feeling energized and full of optimism, and fear.

The following day, I was a bag of nerves in anticipation of our date. One of the other barmen warned me not to get drunk on the first date, because it would probably turn the girl off. I understood what he was saying, but found it hard to drink slowly—especially when I was nervous. He suggested a new strategy: I should order my least favourite drink, and this would discourage me from guzzling too fast. To me, this sounded like a good plan. Cider reminded me of being sick when I first started drinking, so cider was my drink of choice on that first date.

I had arranged to meet *Lucy* in a bar next to Goodge street tube station in London. I got there a bit early so I could have a pint to soothe my nerves. I drank the cider that I ordered much quicker than I had intended, and ended up thinking that it wasn't so bad after all. Starting on my second pint, I had to force myself to slow down. I was still nervous, and convinced myself that she wouldn't show up. Maybe she'd had second thoughts or had been trying to make a fool out of me. Like I'd thought, she was way out of my league. Why would she want to waste her time with a loser like me? These worries had crossed my mind throughout the day—now it was a certainty. I wasn't too devastated though. The cider was going down nicely and I figured that if she didn't turn up, I would have a bloody good drink to massage my wounded pride. But *Lucy* did show up, and she turned out to be great company. I did end up drinking too much, but she didn't seem to mind.

LUCY AND I soon became a couple. She'd sometimes stay in my room above the bar, but most often we stayed in her student accommodation. I preferred staying at her place because visitors weren't meant to be in the students' rooms overnight and finding ways of sneaking in became part of the fun. Sometimes this would involve climbing in through windows on the ground floor while other times she would open the fire door for me and we would just leg it to her room laughing all the way as the alarms blared around us.

Lucy didn't seem too bothered with my lack of future prospects and was accepting of my dysfunctional lifestyle. I, on the other hand, became even more depressed about my lack of qualifications. It's difficult to explain the contradictions I experienced at this time in my life. On the one hand, I felt threatened by her student friends who seemed to have so much more going for them than I did, and on the other hand, I told myself that I was living the good life and they didn't know what they were talking about. I was never a violent drunk, but I could get extremely vicious verbally when full of booze. I'd sometimes end up mocking her and her university friends—this nasty side of my personality must have been highly unattractive. Still, *Lucy* was very understanding and she tolerated my outbursts and petty jealousies.

One day she suggested that I try going back to education. This was something which I hadn't really considered, but the idea filled me with enthusiasm. It seemed like the perfect solution to all my problems. Maybe it would be possible for me to enter the world of academia after all, and no longer be a jealous outsider. It also demonstrated that she believed in me, in my potential. I hoped to rid myself of my feelings of inferiority and already I was imagining discussing serious topics with friends in bars after class. I had sunk so low into my addiction at this point that bars were the only places I could envisage—I never went anywhere else. In my mind, this seemed like a great step in my personal development. I was feeling so motivated that I immediately began to make plans and accumulate the necessary information. I arranged to go back and do my A Levels once the next term began, and I also got a new job packing shelves on the night-shift in Tescos, which left me free to study during the day.

WE WERE GOING out together almost a year when *Lucy* invited me to Liverpool to meet her family. The chance to leave London for a few days excited me. Even though it would be a bit nerve-wracking, I looked forward to meeting her parents. Our relationship seemed serious and maybe this was the time to take it to the next level; I felt ready to make a commitment to her for the rest of my life.

We arrived in *Lucy*'s hometown, and as usual the first thing that I wanted to do was check out the local bars. Maybe that mythical venue that I'd been searching for would be in Liverpool. Visiting somewhere new and not checking out its drinking establishments seemed completely unorthodox to me. I explained to *Lucy* that I needed to calm my nerves and how getting along with people felt so much easier with a drink inside me.

I wanted her family to like me after all. She reminded me that we'd already had a few cans on the train. After a bit of cajoling, she dropped me off at a nearby bar. I realise now, though at the time I didn't see it, that I was driven to want to drink out of fear. I was afraid to confront my problem, afraid to meet new people, afraid of the unknown. Bars offered me familiarity and a place to be myself.

We spent two days in Liverpool, with me spending as much of the time as possible getting drunk. *Lucy* was annoyed, and any attempts she made to put restrictions on my drinking just irritated me greatly. I was actually spending much less time in the pub than I wanted, and such was my twisted logic that I was annoyed for not getting any credit for this sacrifice. The thoughts of spending a sober afternoon with my possible future in-laws, on their territory, seemed like torture to me. As pleasant and welcoming as her family were, I'd much rather spend my time with an ice cold pint than conversing with them. I left Liverpool happily deluded that it had been a successful trip and that the family had liked me. However, *Lucy* was quick to correct this misconception on the train by telling me that her mum had warned her that my drinking seemed out of control, and that it would all end in tears. Whenever I was confronted like this about my addiction, I went into denial and this time was no different. I sulked after hearing this 'unfair assessment' of my character, and didn't realise that this incident was to mark the beginning of the end of our relationship.

Over the next few weeks *Lucy* distanced herself from me, but the more she pulled away, the more I tried to hold on. I became clingy and needy. I turned to my favourite drug, and became verbally abusive more frequently. Of course, this didn't help our relationship and we argued constantly. We began spending less time together because *Lucy* said she needed to study, and when I'd try to call her I'd usually receive the news that she wasn't in her room. From my perspective I was about to turn a new corner in my life—a new job, going back to education—and I was hoping she would be there for me through all this. I had wanted us to move in together, but now I would be moving to a bed-sit alone. *Lucy* claimed that the new place was too far from university.

Then one day, she confronted me with the news that she needed a break from me. It was near to the end of her course and she told me that needed to study hard for exams—our relationship was getting in the way. I reacted badly and pleaded pitifully, making all types of promises but she couldn't be swayed. I made angry accusations and she responded by asking me why I expected so much from other people, yet so little from myself. She left me with the promise that maybe once her exams were over we could get back together. I left her room clutching on to this small hope.

FOR SOME REASON this felt much worse than my previous break-ups. I was about to leave my job and start a new life but fear, sadness, and uncertainty made everything appear impossibly daunting. I wallowed in my own self-pity and wondered how *Lucy* could leave me at such a critical stage in my life. I wasn't able to cope and I took my usual escape route: alcohol. I hit it hard. I stopped eating and people began to comment on my physical deterioration. My mood would swing from total apathy to complete despair in the space of a few minutes. My boss informed me one morning that when he first heard that I was thinking of leaving the bar he had wanted to talk me out of it, but now he just wanted me gone. I had become 'a liability' was how he put it. I hated him for saying that even though it was obvious that he was right. I collapsed behind the bar one night and my only concern was that *Lucy* might hear the news and come running. She didn't.

I hadn't seen *Lucy* in over a week despite my best efforts to bump into her, when one afternoon I saw her walking past the bar. I ran out after her and she seemed genuinely shocked by the state I was in but she agreed to meet up for a chat. I was delighted because I knew that if we could just talk things over I would be able to convince her that we had a future together. I pinned all my hopes for the future on this meeting.

IN THE EVENINGS we were given an hour's break from the bar, and I always used this opportunity to visit another pub near Oxford Street. On my way back to work after visiting this pub one night, I saw *Lucy*. She was on the opposite side of the road with a man who had his arm around her. They were both laughing. I called out her name and she looked at me with a look of shock which soon turned into a 'well-now-you-know' expression. She didn't say anything and the man that was with her just gave me a smile. I returned to the bar and knocked back pint after pint until reaching the welcome numbness of a blackout.

The next day I made the decision to go back to Ireland. There was no way that I could begin a new job and return to education with my head in such a mess. The people around me seemed relieved with this decision. A part of me hoped that *Lucy* would see this as a complete 'fuck you'. I had never felt so betrayed, though now I can see that I was the one doing the betraying.

CHAPTER 11

WHEN MY RELATIONSHIP with *Lucy* ended I had been close to a mental breakdown, but I had managed to somehow keep it together. Two years later, however, my mind finally snapped, but this time, it wasn't because of a woman. In fact, when the breakdown happened my life actually seemed to be going in the right direction, and I was very close to achieving my goal of entering university.

I spent a few months back in Dublin licking my wounds after the split with *Lucy*, then I found myself back in London and working in Waterloo. I had let my hair grow to below my shoulders, but more productively, I had found my way back into education. I studied for the A Levels through distance learning while also working in a bar. My dream had been to attend classes and to have student friends, but my work schedule wouldn't allow for this. Still, this studying by correspondence did have its advantages. I could do it in my own time and still earn enough money to have a great social life.

By the summer of 1994 I had obtained the necessary qualifications to begin a degree in Social Science. I had managed to pass my exams and complete the coursework despite the fact that my alcohol intake remained out of control. I seldom studied sober and would forget most of what I read, but somehow I muddled through. My results were far from impressive, but they were sufficient to get me into the next level of education. For perhaps the first time in my life, I felt proud of myself.

Nevertheless, 1994 was also a year when I felt close to insanity. My mind would sometimes feel so out of control that suicide seemed to be the only solution. I thought about it the whole time. The idea of ending it all excited me, and the only time that I'd feel really alive was when planning my own demise. Life seemed far less hostile when planning to escape it. The idea of death had always haunted me, but it wasn't dying that frightened me, just my powerlessness to stop it from happening. Suicide felt empowering.

The fact that I had started abusing amphetamines didn't do much to improve my state of mind. I loved speed because it allowed me to drink all night and go to work the next day. That was my purpose in taking it—so that I could drink more. But, while the drug did keep me awake, it also made me paranoid and caused my behaviour to become even more erratic.

At the time I was also a big Nirvana fan and it was around this time that Kurt Cobain, the band's lead singer, took his own life. I admired him for telling the world to 'go fuck itself' and when Nirvana wanted to call their album, 'I hate myself, and want to die', I knew exactly what they meant. More times than I care to remember that year I woke up with a sore neck to find I had a rope tied around it, and a suicide note beside my bed. Then the inevitable finally happened; it was a moment I'd been waiting for my entire life.

MY BREAKDOWN OCCURRED on the day my exam results arrived in the post. I had passed everything and would be able to attend university in a couple of months, but instead of wanting to celebrate, or even feeling a sense of achievement, my mood turned completely black. My thoughts began racing and all I can remember thinking was 'so this is what madness feels like'. I couldn't gain any control over my mind for the next few days; everything went blank and my thoughts were a blur. I couldn't think straight and I started wandering the streets aimlessly. I ended up sleeping rough and begging for money to buy a few cans of cider in the hope that alcohol would help calm my thoughts, as it had so many times before. But this time not even alcohol was working. My thoughts continued to race out of control and I tried to drink myself into a stupor. I ended up sitting under a tunnel in Elephant & Castle, near the university that I had hoped to attend, sitting in my own piss and shit, begging for money, knowing that I wouldn't be going to university anytime soon. This period of my life fills me with shame, but at the time I was beyond caring.

I remember vividly walking around London during that period hoping that somebody would notice the mess I was in and take me to a hospital. The days of feeling worried that people might think I was crazy were gone. I couldn't have cared less about what people thought; I just wanted the pain in my head to stop. I wanted to be admitted to hospital but felt too out of control to do this myself; the idea of having to answer questions filled me with more despair. Nobody tried to help me though, so I waited for my thoughts to settle enough to be able to admit myself. I felt so desperate and helpless. I would have jumped off a bridge but this required too much energy. I was too afraid to talk to people in shops or bars, so I couldn't even buy alcohol anymore.

I somehow ended up walking in the New Cross area and found myself outside the Alcohol Recovery Project (ARP) office. I mustered up the strength and presence of mind to go in. The people there sat me down, and I managed to convey to them how fucked up I felt. I was a total mess; my clothes were dirty, and I must have smelt revolting, but they spent a long time talking to me and made me feel a bit better. They said that I would have to enter their detox programme, but they didn't have a place for me that day.

I had already gone for more than 36 hours without alcohol, and apparently this was the most dangerous time during detoxification. The ARP had a dry-house for those who had passed through detox. Initially they wanted me to admit myself to hospital but after further discussion they told me that if I managed to stay sober for the rest of the week, I could go straight to their dry-house. This suggestion helped to soothe my troubled mind. I wasn't capable of making rational decisions for myself anymore and I was relieved to be able to turn my life over to someone else. We came to an arrangement whereby they would monitor my condition during the day, and I would attend AA meetings in the evening.

I was dangerously close to death and the ARP sent me for a check-up with a doctor who was connected to their organisation. He was young and friendly and he wasn't judgmental about the mess I had made of my life. He diagnosed me with alcohol induced depression and told me that I needed to enter treatment. He too wasn't comfortable with the idea of me going through detox alone, warning me that withdrawal symptoms could be fatal and that there was still a danger after the first 72 hours, but I had no other option.

That evening I attended an AA meeting. I sat shaking near the back of the room and was terrified that somebody might ask me to speak. The sober people around me seemed so healthy, which just made me feel dirtier and all the more unworthy of being there. But I no longer felt as though I were too good to be in AA. I just wanted the madness to stop and for my brain to slow down. I wanted to be normal like everyone else; I wanted to have a life. What I had now couldn't be called a life. After the meeting people did speak to me, but they seemed to understand my delicate state of mind and weren't too pushy. They just wanted to make sure that I was okay and to let me know that AA was there for me.

At the time I was renting a cockroach infested room above a launderette off the Old Kent Road. I decided to spend the night there rather than wandering the streets. That night was horrendous. Alcohol withdrawal kicked in, and I spent the whole night shaking and hallucinating. There were cockroaches everywhere, and I was unable to distinguish between the ones which actually existed and those that were just in my mind. In the depths of my nightmare, I felt as if insects were crawling all over me and I kept swatting different parts of my body to beat them off. I was on the verge of a panic attack the entire time. I was utterly alone and I was terrified.

The next morning I returned to the ARP office and told them there was no way that I could stay in my room one night longer. As this was my fourth day off alcohol I was through the acute withdrawal stage. They agreed to let me enter the dry-house a couple of days early. I was overwhelmed with gratitude. I went back to my shitty bed-sit and just grabbed the bare necessities to take with me; I was afraid of transferring the cockroaches to my new location. I never wanted to see one of those disgusting creatures again. I also left most of my CDs behind. My music collection was very strongly associated with my being messed-up and I wanted a new start with no ghosts from the past dragging me down.

CHAPTER 12

THE PURPOSE OF the dry-house was to provide a therapeutic environment where recovering alcoholics could get their lives back together. I would be expected to stay there for up to a year. The dry-house itself was situated on a nice middle-class street in Catford. The house looked anonymous from the outside and showed no signs that a group of recovering drunks lived inside the building. It was certainly a step-up from my decrepit room on the Old Kent Road. The house was very orderly and clean, which I found comforting. Nothing was out of place and it felt like a proper home. For years I'd been living in bed-sits and bar accommodation and, with the exception of my occasional sabbaticals in Ireland, there were no home comforts in my life.

My new housemates and I exchanged our life stories, and our pasts turned out to be quite similar. The other residents varied in age from a man in his 60s to three guys in their 20s. The youngest was a 20-year-old, and when he left the following week, I became the youngest of the group. We sat around a wooden table in the kitchen drinking coffee. We had a good laugh at each other's tales of woe—it wasn't a mean-spirited laugh, but one which came from empathy and understanding. People who have never had a drug or alcohol addiction can be very sympathetic, but they just can't comprehend what it is actually like. It felt so good to laugh again, and it made all my problems seem much more manageable. We understood each other's misery perfectly because we had all been there. We could laugh at the hell we had been through.

My previous reservations towards AA now vanished. I threw myself fully into the organisation. New members are encouraged to attend 90 meetings in 90 days, but I almost doubled this. The doctor had arranged a disability pass for me so that I could travel to meetings on the London buses and trains for free. This helped significantly and it really increased my participation in the group. Previously I went from bar to bar so it was easy to fall into the habit of trying out different meetings.

We did activities and group work in the house most days. I soon became familiar with spending most of the day discussing my previous drinking problem and current recovery. One day I met an old friend who had also quit drinking; he warned me that spending so much time focused on not drinking seemed a bit extreme. I didn't care though, I was too afraid of a return to addiction to do anything else.

I am not sure what the situation is now, but in the mid-90s there were thousands of AA meetings around

London. I had been given a thick booklet at my first meeting which listed all the groups and the times the meetings began. I took this guidebook everywhere along with an A to Z map of London. There seemed to be an AA meeting to cater for every segment of society that you could imagine. I mostly went to the smaller meetings because it was easier to make friends. But I also liked to attend the young people's meetings because, although I was now 25 years old, I still sometimes felt young when compared to the average AA member. The rich meetings could be fun and it was common to see famous celebrities who would remind us that we were all in this together. AA soon felt like a family.

Since my initial foray into AA back in Dublin all those years ago, my attitude towards it had completely changed. I became 100% convinced that they offered the only solution for drunks. The AA message seemed simple to me: do it our way or you will return to alcohol, and it will be worse next time. That had certainly been my own experience. I was in a far worse state now than the first time I attended AA at the age of 20, and the idea of returning to a life of drinking, and to possibly descend even further into addiction, scared the shit out of me.

Not everyone in the dry-house believed the AA message, however, and, in the beginning, I was the only one attending. I became a bit of a fanatic and worried that it was only a matter of time before my housemates would drink again unless they got on the programme. I often got into heated debates with them when I started banging on about AA. Still, after a few days in the house, one of them noticed that it did seem to be helping me, and he too became fanatical about the meetings.

Within a few weeks of quitting alcohol my mind completely cleared. As well as going to meetings I also started to get back into shape physically. I began swimming and tried a bit of kickboxing until I eventually found my way into a tai chi class. I'd missed martial arts a lot so it felt like coming home. Tai chi was an ideal way to re-introduce myself to this type of disciplined practice. The move away from martial arts had been the start of my problems so the move back to it felt completely appropriate.

I liked sharing the house with a group of other sober people. We would stay up late at night discussing our future plans, and with cutting honesty, we would describe our past experiences. We found hope from one another and pulled each other through the difficult days. Our conversations were like none that I had encountered before; I admitted things to these people that would have been unthinkable for me to share in the past. The strange thing was that when my dark secrets were out in the open they didn't appear so diabolical. They were actually quite tame when compared to some of the other people's confessions.

We would have group meetings most days, and once a week we had one-to-one meetings with our house-worker. She was also an ex-alcoholic who had been sober for over 12 years, and she served not only as a wise counsel but also as an inspiration. She seemed to really understand where I was coming from and I always felt comfortable talking to her, as she had gone through similar experiences.

We went through a phase of having explosive meetings in the house and each of us experienced periods where we isolated ourselves from the rest of the group. In the beginning I loved being involved with everyone, but it could be challenging because we were all selfish alcoholics who had spent years being self-absorbed and secretive. When one of us started to become isolated, the rest of the group would use the meetings to ask what was happening. It felt very threatening, but I soon learned that it was necessary, because the first sign of an impending relapse in the dry-houses was to stop being involved in group sessions, and to begin avoiding other housemates.

Our biggest fear in the house was that one of us would drink again. We had all heard stories about other dry-houses where one of the residents started drinking again, and before you knew it, everyone in the house was back drinking. I cherished my sobriety, but I didn't completely trust myself not to drink if those around me relapsed. We all got a bit paranoid when anyone started acting differently because of the danger that they were back on the sauce. As soon as someone was caught drinking they were out.

The first person in the house to relapse was *Lorento*. He was an Italian in his 60s but had lived in England for over 30 years. He still maintained a slight Italian accent but claimed that he had almost completely forgotten his native tongue. He told stories which were sometimes hard to believe but always great fun to hear. *Lorento*'s tall stocky frame and booming voice made him the centre of attention in any room. When he joined us in group, or for a cup of coffee, he would always clap his hands loudly as he entered the room, calling out 'Hello boys' cheerily. We all liked him and looked upon *Lorento* as a great source of entertainment.

Lorento frequently expressed his belief that the dry-house was his last chance in life and that there was no way that he was going to waste it. The rest of us would have times when it all became too much, but *Lorento* always seemed to be positive. On low days it would be to him that I would turn for advice. The first hint that things weren't going as smoothly for him as they seemed was when he lost his temper one day in group for no apparent reason. We'd never seen that side to him before. After that he began to go missing from the house, and one night he returned with glassy eyes and slurred speech. Despite his attempts to mask the smell, it was obvious that he had been drinking. He was asked to leave the house the next day. *Lorento*'s relapse elicited a mix of emotions from me: sadness that he had probably blown his last chance, anger that he had fooled me, but mostly, fear that it might happen to me too.

IF WE MANAGED to stay sober for a year in the programme we would be rewarded with a council house or flat. Accommodation like this was hard to come by in London. There were rumours of ARP residents who had only joined the programme with the intention of staying sober for a year so that they could get a flat and save some money for their next round on the booze. An older man from one of the other houses confided in me that he had no intention of staying sober once he had left his dry-house. Most ARP residents came from the streets and knew exactly how the welfare system worked. Others weren't even prepared to wait the year and would attempt to get their entire house to relapse in the hope that a united group of active drunks would be able to fool the case-workers and counsellors.

I wanted my own recovery to last but worried about relapse all the time. My sleep was frequently disturbed by nightmares that I was back on the booze. People would tell me that I'd need to actually decide to return to alcohol, but I also heard stories in AA meetings about those who suddenly found themselves in a bar drinking and wondering how the hell they got there. This scared the shit out of me. The AA believed that a return to drink usually occurred once people stopped attending meetings and sharing their problems. AA meetings were often compared to money in the bank, and that it was important to have as much in your account as possible. I made sure to go to at least one AA meeting every day.

Amazing things happened when I attended AA meetings and socialised with AA members. I never felt as close to anyone as I did in the meetings. The other members could see through my bullshit, so there was no point in hiding anything, and they understood exactly where I was coming from. Many of the old-timers in AA had this special glow—they called it serenity. These guys had conquered their addiction and they had finally found peace. They claimed to feel content all the time, and I didn't doubt them. I began to be proud of being an AA member and to think that being an alcoholic might actually be a blessing because it had brought me into AA, and offered me the perfect philosophy to live by. AA also hosted many social functions for us to enjoy: conventions, parties, and even dances. I had never danced sober in my adult life, and it took some coaxing for me to do it initially. When I finally did, however, it felt wonderfully liberating. This convinced me further that a life without alcohol actually was possible and could perhaps be even more enjoyable than the life of a drunk. This revelation, as foolish as it may sound, was actually an earth-shattering experience for me. I had never thought that way before. Previous to this experience I had always firmly believed that alcohol added positively to my life.

IT WAS A rule at the dry-house that we had to remain on long-term sickness benefit while on the programme so full-time work was out of the question. My house-worker suggested that I try some voluntary work. She convinced me that this would be a good way for me to find my way back into the world of employment. I still intended to go to university at some stage, but for the time being, voluntary work would allow me to feel that I was being useful, instead of just being an unemployed recovering alcoholic. I hoped such work would be a road to Damascus experience.

I began helping out at a homeless shelter called St Martin in the Fields. This work brought me back in contact with active alcoholism. I could now appreciate the waste of human life that resulted from addiction and I had to fight the urge to try and save everybody around me. I remembered that the last thing I wanted to hear when I was drinking was some ex-drunk lecturing me on the benefits of sobriety, so instead of trying to actively convert people, I just let it be known that I was a recovering alcoholic and that they could approach me any time for a chat if they wanted to.

The house-worker also found an organisation that catered for people with learning difficulties. I hadn't considered this type of work and was hesitant at first, but I didn't want to appear lazy or ungrateful so I agreed to give it a shot. During my meeting with a worker from the organisation I learnt that some of the clients had quite profound disabilities. I had no idea how I would cope with this and I was worried about letting my house-worker down.

They suggested that I start off by spending some time with one of their clients. His name was Paul, like me.

He had no family, and the organisation felt that Paul would benefit from some contact with people other than his paid carers. He had serious disabilities which left him completely wheelchair bound and with very limited movement throughout his body. Paul could barely communicate and relied completely on other people to take care of his daily needs.

On my way to visit him for the first time I had to stop myself from turning around and going back to the dry-house. My apprehensions only increased further while I was waiting to meet him. I was told that his carers were getting him ready and I was asked to wait in the living room. The house had a homely and modern feel to it but certain adaptations had been made to meet the unique needs of the residents. There were items which I associated with hospitals scattered around with normal household items and the smells and noises were strange and unfamiliar to me.

I instinctively glanced through the video collection which surrounded the television on shelves. It mostly consisted of cartoons and a music collection of children's songs and golden oldies. My browsing was interrupted by someone screaming in another part of the house and at this point I seriously considered fleeing. What had I gotten myself into? At that moment, a young woman wearing her pyjamas came into the room. She shuffled along with her knees turned inward and her head leaned to one side. She gave me a big smile and didn't seem in the least bit surprised to find me in her sitting room. She immediately began chatting to me, firing questions at me but showing no interest in my answers. She kept repeating the same questions, but the distraction put me at ease and I was glad of her company.

Paul was wheeled into the room a few minutes later. We were introduced, and my namesake gave me a lopsided grin. The carer told me that Paul liked to have his head rubbed but the thought of rubbing another man's head initially repelled me. I felt uncomfortable with the idea of physical contact and I considered just saying no to it or pretending not to have heard, but I worried that this might make me seem hard-hearted or weak. I awkwardly began moving my hand through Paul's hair. He made loud 'hrrr' sounds which I found a bit off-putting and after a few seconds I stopped, but Paul grabbed my hand again in order for me to continue. I focused on the task of just rubbing his head and soon forgot my own discomfort. The carer then asked me to help put on Paul's shoes. His feet were quite badly deformed and getting the shoes on involved a lot of twisting and turning, so much so in fact that I worried I might hurt him.

The purpose of my visit had been to take Paul out of the house for a few hours, but now that he was in front of me, this seemed like a huge responsibility. What if something went wrong? I knew nothing about taking care of people with special needs, I could barely take care of myself. I asked the care worker about what I should do if something happened while we were away from the house. She assured me that all would be fine, but suggested that, as it was our first time together, we should just go for a walk around the nearby park. That way if something did go wrong, we would be able to return home quickly.

The journey around the park passed uneventfully. Paul seemed pleased with the wind in his face and the change of scenery. The park was teeming with activity. I hardly ever visited parks, but I enjoyed the stroll so much that I promised myself to visit them more often. I brought Paul for three laps of the park. The day was cold, and I began to worry that he might be feeling uncomfortable, but it was hard for me to judge how cold it actually was because pushing the chair kept me warm. Nevertheless, I decided it was time to take him back.

I returned to the dry-house filled with a sense of accomplishment and I realised that doing something for somebody else came with a reward. I hadn't done anything special, but it had been a change from my normal self-centred behaviour. I was certain that I had benefited more from the experience than Paul had, and one of my housemates remarked that I looked relaxed and content.

I continued to spend time with Paul and it turned out to be a life-changing experience for me. My weekly visits to him always left me with a sense of calm. I had spent too much time locked in my own internal prison where I had played the role of both prisoner and jailer. Thinking about somebody else, even just for a couple of hours a week, helped to put my own life into perspective. I realised that I wasn't alone in finding life difficult, and that I wasn't being picked on by some higher power. Compared to Paul's challenges my own problems seemed trivial and I began to see that helping others benefited the giver at least as much as the receiver.

I began reading up in the library on the subject of learning difficulties. I was greatly affected by a novel called *Skallagirgg* by William Horwood. This story was based on people with learning difficulties, and despite being a work of fiction, it really made me think about how it might feel to have a disability.

My new state of mind began to affect my overall demeanour and this was noticeable to those around me. My housemates admitted that previously I had seemed moody and somewhat arrogant, but that I now appeared happier and more approachable. My counsellor also praised my progress, and I did feel that something had changed significantly inside me. I believed that along with AA and ARP, the time spent with Paul had a lot to do these changes and for perhaps the first time in my life I felt truly alive.

THE SPIRITUAL ASPECTS of the AA programme interested me greatly, and I felt that in order to maintain my sobriety, I would need to cultivate my spiritual side. I began attending the meetings which focused more on the 12 steps. I didn't want to belong to any 'God Squad', and my doubts regarding Christianity hadn't changed, but I could see the benefits of following a spiritual path. I was now able to separate spirituality from religious dogma and focused on living a life based on improving as a person.

It was also around this time, on a bus going from Bromley to the house back in Catford, that I had a rather unusual experience. I was sitting on the top floor of a red London bus, just gazing out the window and my mind was content and relaxed. I felt at ease to be just sitting there and in no rush to get home. I was happy to sit and enjoy the beautiful sunny day as it passed before me. Suddenly, my perceptions shifted, and for a few seconds I felt connected to everything around me. A warm yellow glow seemed to fill the bus, and for the first time in my life there was no fear in my mind. I understood that I was part of something far bigger and that 'I' no longer mattered. More importantly, it didn't matter that I didn't matter. I felt as though my mind was expanding and that it might burst with sheer delight.

I had hallucinated previously on drugs but this experience was nothing like that. This felt 100% real, like the most real thing I had ever experienced. The feeling left almost as soon as it had come, but it didn't matter. I knew that what had happened might be a once-off phenomenon, but I also knew that it would stay with me forever. I basked in the afterglow of this experience for days afterwards, and even now I find it comforting to think back on this episode.

Perhaps I felt moved because of my friend Paul. In time I came to realise the time I spent with him had allowed me to reach a decision which I would not have considered prior to meeting him. In fact, I probably would have laughed at the idea. I decided that I wanted to become a nurse. This decision made sense for me and answered the question that was always niggling away at the back of my mind about what I should do with my life. I informed the house-worker about my plan and she was very supportive, saying she believed this to be further evidence of how well I was doing in recovery.

MY YEAR AT the dry-house came to an end and the counsellor decided that I was ready to be returned to the real world. I would be given an apartment that would be mine to live in for the rest of my life, if I wanted it. There was even the option of half-rent and half-mortgage so that I would eventually own it. As well as a new home I was also to be given a grant of £1,000 to buy some furniture.

I knew that moving out of the dry-house into our own place was the most dangerous time for those on the ARP programme. I had already witnessed one guy relapse as soon as he got his new home and was given a big wad of cash, and I had heard about many more, though I didn't worry too much about my own sobriety. I felt strong, and others assured me that AA meetings would keep me that way. I did still miss alcohol sometimes, but I could see how a life without it had many advantages. I worried that maybe at some future date my determination to stay sober might desert me, but for the moment I was confident.

I realised my ambition to become a nurse when I got accepted to St Bartholomew's School of Nursing. I devoted the next three years of my life to gaining a qualification which would allow me entry into the nursing profession. I hoped it would be a bridge to my living a more dynamic, real life and I no longer wanted a life based around making myself numb to the world.

CHAPTER 13

I MANAGED TO stay sober for two years. I lasted almost six months into my nursing training before deciding to drink again. People who knew me at the time were shocked when they heard the news that I was back on the bottle, my life had seemed to be going so well. When asked to provide some justification for it I struggled to explain it. I suppose at the end of the day it all boiled down to my 'fuck it button'.

The fuck-it button was something that formed an important part of my drinking habits from the very beginning. The mental process that always led me to this reaction is easy to understand in hindsight. At the time, however, it was overwhelming. My life could be going fine, then suddenly I'd be hit with a feeling of utter helplessness. I'd think, well what's the point of it all? Sure, staying sober means my life runs more smoothly, but it also means deprivation, and losing out on the high that comes with inebriation. I'd figure I was going to die anyway so why not just party, party, party? Another familiar train of thought which always led me to the bottle was: 'I was born an alcoholic so why fight nature?'

Looking back it is easy to see the warning signs that suggested I was at risk of relapsing, but at the time it was not obvious to me. One early sign was that I began to find the AA meetings irritating. I was proud of my achievements since becoming sober, but people in the meetings constantly reminded me that 'I owed it all to AA.' My pride found this more and more difficult to accept. I thought, 'Fuck that, it was me doing all the work.'

On top of that, some of the people in AA, who had been in it for years, weren't as well or as righteous as they claimed. I'd hear members say all the right things in the meetings then make racist or negative comments outside. I resented being lectured by people who I thought were insincere and two-faced.

As my discomfort with AA continued, I saw less of the success stories and more of the people who were still struggling after years of being sober, as well as those who sounded somewhat less than honest. Even the serene old-timers began to annoy me. I found their constant repetition of the AA slogans irritating, and I thought they were out of touch with reality.

AA was losing its magic touch for me, and I became more and more disillusioned with it, or should I say I wanted to become disillusioned with it. Most of the members were middle-aged or older, and even though I knew rationally that getting sober at a young age meant that I had a chance of living a full life, it just seemed to be unfair. I envied those who had had years of drinking behind them before going into recovery. I began to believe that my addiction had never been bad enough to warrant lifelong abstinence. A common saying in AA was, 'If you can't remember your last drink then you haven't had it yet.' I couldn't remember my last drink because my mind had been so messed up at the time, so maybe there were more drinks to come.

I'd also begun to question the seriousness of my previous problems with alcohol. I'd met people whose drinking had caused the death of another, and others who'd drink boot polish in a desperate bid to get drunk. I had been messed up mentally, but nowhere near as bad as some alcoholics. Another young member summed it up perfectly in a meeting one day when he said: 'Some of you are here for mass murder, while some of us are only here for parking violations.' I hoped I belonged to this second category.

ON TOP OF being sober for almost two years, I had also been celibate. This arrangement had suited me for a long time, but then I began to miss being intimate with the opposite sex. There were women in AA, but romance between members was discouraged because it apparently doubled your risk of relapse. Besides, there was no way that I wanted a relationship with someone as fucked-up as I was. I found it difficult to chat up women when sober, and this caused me to worry whether a sober life meant sacrificing my sex life. I had met a few people in recovery who hadn't had sex in years, and were proverbially dry-humping lampposts. I didn't want to end up like that.

But what really triggered my drinking again was the feeling of missing out on something. I had worked for years to be able to attend university and now that I'd achieved that goal, I felt that I was entitled to live the student life, the life that involved sitting in bars, and having intelligent discussions over cold pints of beer. My fellow student nurses all seemed to be having a great time of it and sitting with them in the pubs, sipping on a coke, didn't make me feel part of the group. I missed the wild old days when most of the drinking was done with me leading the charge.

The truth was that I missed alcohol and I constantly thought back to the days when I had really enjoyed having a few drinks—the days in Oxford and those early drinking years in Dublin. 'Romancing the drink' is what they called this in the meetings, and even though I knew about this tendency, I felt helpless to stop it. I couldn't control the thoughts that entered my head and if relapse was going to happen anyway, I figured why bother fighting it.

Of course, I knew I was playing Russian Roulette, and despite all the different factors that led me back to booze, none of my excuses could justify it. I knew the risks: I risked experiencing the mental torture that had led me to seek recovery in the first place all over again, and I risked losing all the good that had come into my life. And for what? For a chemical which numbed my brain for a few hours, and which brought far more pain than pleasure into my life. But I just thought 'fuck it'. Maybe I didn't deserve to have good things in my life.

I was tired of being an alcoholic. I was tired of being in recovery. I was tired of feeling like a victim of this 'deadly disease'. I was tired of living in fear of the day that I might relapse. I wanted to overcome this problem and live like the people I considered to be normal, those who enjoyed the occasional drink, and didn't have to confess their every thought to a group of strangers in a recovery group.

ON THAT AFTERNOON, when I ordered my first drink since becoming sober, I just didn't want to have to argue with that part of my brain that missed alcohol anymore. Even as the drink went down my throat, a part of me was screaming 'Are you really doing this?' But once it was done, it was done. The next morning I felt full of remorse and would have done almost anything to turn the clock back, but the decision had been made and now I had to pay the price. I hoped that I would return to recovery eventually, but I never expected that it would only happen ten misery-filled years later.

CHAPTER 14

I HAD BEEN back drinking for a few weeks, and in my mind, things didn't seem to be so bad. I hadn't immediately collapsed into the mess I had been a few years earlier and it felt great to be a part of the student social scene. Drinking renewed my confidence with women, and I started having sex again. I was able to limit myself to a couple of pints a night at the start, but as my confidence grew, so did the amount I drank. I had made good friends with the small group of non-drinkers on the course, but I soon replaced these companions with more hardened drinkers.

Just a few years previously I'd been so envious of the students who I'd served drinks to, but now I was the one sitting in bars with my university friends, discussing subjects which had once seemed so fascinating and alien to me. We had these beer-fuelled chats at least three times a week after class. Occasionally we would be joined by our professors who would give impromptu lectures in the Barley Mow pub for as long as we fawned over them. Not only did they provide this extra-tuition for free, but they would even buy us a pint if we were lucky. I hated sitting through lectures, learning was much more pleasant when I had a pint in front of me. Now that I was a student, I had access to the Student Union bars and the cheap alcohol within. I had been so intrigued by these places when I had worked near University College London but I could never gain admission to them.

I gave up my apartment because the nursing accommodation was cheaper and provided more opportunity to find drinking buddies. Everyone said that I was mad to give up council accommodation when so many were desperate for this type of housing in London. They warned me that it would be almost impossible to obtain a property like this again. But my mind was made up and I couldn't be swayed. To be honest, I felt guilty about still staying there as it had been given to me as a reward for staying sober. The apartment only acted as a reminder of my failure.

I managed to complete my three years of training despite being back on the drink. I passed every assessment first time, and I never missed a day from my work placements. I got by on doing the bare minimum, however.

As time went by my drinking became heavier and heavier, and my relationships with my classmates became strained, but I was dedicated enough to achieving my goals not to lose control completely. You might say that instead of enhancing my student experience, alcohol was clearly diminishing it. I'd make an attempt to stop every few months, but I failed each time.

On the positive side of things, I did seem to have the makings of a good nurse. I walked straight into employment on a ward where I had been a student after finishing my training. I took the job seriously and did my best not to allow alcohol to interfere with my work. I felt proud to be a qualified nurse and the worst of my drinking occurred on my days off.

The job was fine, but I began to grow tired of living in London. Once again alcohol was having a depressive effect on my mind so everything around me looked bleak. I blamed my unfriendly neighbours, and the gloomy streets of London for getting me down. Of course, I was being 'geographical' again. I believed that if I moved, my life would improve, in spite of the fact that this had never worked in the past, and so, I went travelling around Europe as often as possible. I was still searching for the perfect bar, but now my pub crawls were occurring in places like Berlin and Tallinn. These trips would briefly lift my spirits, but as soon as I returned to London my depression would descend upon me once more. Eventually I decided to take my show back on the road.

I RETURNED TO Oxford, the source of so many of my earlier happy memories, in a bid to lift my depression. I got work in one of the major hospitals there, and soon found myself surrounded by new drinking buddies. For a time, drinking became fun again. I was having a lot of success with women too, and found myself in another relationship. The move to Oxford worked initially, yet the novelty soon wore off and I was back to being as depressed as before. My mind and my feelings became dull, I was numbed to reality, and alcohol once more became something I needed just to function, so I turned to travel again in an attempt at lightening my mood. Like all my other addictions, I now had to travel more and more to get the same effect, and I started going further afield: The United States, Jamaica, Asia. I saw very little of the countries I visited—apart from their bars.

I financed these trips through a newly acquired credit card, with no consideration as to how I would pay the money back. Each month I would work a week of nights and on my last night I'd look up cheap holiday deals on the Internet and would be off to the airport as soon as my shift ended. It all felt so spontaneous and exciting. This was how I first ended up in Thailand.

I HAD ALWAYS been intrigued by Thailand because of its connection with Buddhism. I also knew about the infamous sex trade there, which made it popular with tourists, but this aspect never interested me. Despite my willingness to fall to the depths of depravity in other areas of my life, I always felt a bit prudish around prostitution.

Bangkok completely dazzled me. I had read Alex Garland's *The Beach* prior to arriving which had amplified my curiosity and fascination with this land that was so foreign and strange to me. I spent my first night in Thailand on the Khao San Road in Bangkok; the starting point for most backpackers in Southeast Asia. I found a cheap room, dumped my belongings and hit the streets straight away. The heat was so strong it felt tangible. I moved from bar to bar, easily falling into conversations with other foreigners who were just as enthralled by the city as I was. All the travellers and backpackers I met on my first day had been travelling for extended periods, and I enjoyed listening to their tales. I could have listened to people talking about the places they had been for the whole night, but jetlag and drunkenness caught up with me, and I called it a night.

On the advice of other travellers I made my way to the island of Koh Pha Ngan the next day. This was one of the places mentioned in *The Beach*. I got burnt on the boat trip over to the island but luckily it looked more painful that it actually was, and it turned out to be a good conversation starter: 'What the fuck happened to you?' I stayed in a resort which charged the equivalent of a few pounds a room per night. The room was actually a dilapidated shed, but I knew that slumming it was all part of the exoticism of travelling in Thailand. The breathtaking scenery more than made up for my meagre accommodation. Looking at the view from the cabin, tears welled up inside me. I had never seen anywhere so beautiful. I spent the next ten days getting drunk and stoned with some gap-year students who were using the resort as a place to recuperate after months of travelling. At the end of my holiday they continued their travels, and I would have done almost anything to have joined them.

After a week, I returned to England determined to take at least a year off to go travelling. My mounting debt needed to be sorted out first, however, and I cashed in my NHS pension, but this barely made a dent in my debt. I felt trapped, with no idea how to escape from my life, until somebody suggested I work my way around the world. I decided to move abroad to some place where I could earn more money before taking time out to travel. At first I considered the States, but the process was taking so long that I abandoned it for Saudi Arabia. The job in Saudi held other attractions for me too. By this stage I was once again sinking into the abyss of alcoholism and my attempts to get sober were becoming more and more fraught. Every couple of months I'd become motivated to stop and would remain dry for a week or so, but then I'd give in to the constant cravings, and the process would start all over again. Alcohol was illegal in Saudi, and I badly wanted the chance to stay sober long enough for my body to recuperate, but as far as I was concerned, this sobriety was to be temporary. When I resumed my travels, I would then be free to hit the bottle as hard as I liked. This future return to heavy drinking was my only motivation in trying to sober up temporarily.

So I applied to an agency that dealt with recruitment for Saudi, and was told that there was plenty of work available, but that the paper work would take a few months to get sorted out. I decided to return to Thailand in the meantime, and use up the remaining credit on my visa card.

I RECEIVED THE news that my grandmother had died shortly before I left for Thailand. We had been very close, and she had played an important role in my life. She had helped to raise me, and my sisters especially, after our parents separated. I thought I would have been completely devastated about it, and while I was really upset upon first hearing the news it became easier to accept after a few days because my mind was already all over the place. It was my normal habit to turn any tragedy into a reason to get and stay drunk, making it all about me so I decided not to return to Ireland for the funeral. I didn't see how my being there would help my grandmother now. I knew I wouldn't be able to handle dealing with my mother at such a difficult time. Selfish as usual, I made the decision to go ahead with my trip to Thailand.

I had intended to spend just a few days back on the Thai islands before travelling around the rest of Southeast Asia, but world cup fever won me over, or more to the point, football gave me an excuse to sit in bars drinking all day. I stayed in the cheapest accommodation that I could find and just partied for the next couple of months.

CHAPTER 15

I HAD ASSUMED that the final part of my application process to work in Saudi would be just a formality. I had hoped to finish everything while still in Thailand, but I was forced to return home for a medical and to receive my visa. I arrived back in Ireland with a nice tan, and with my addiction to alcohol as potent as ever. I arranged the medical check-up straight away and went along to a local doctor's office where everything went smoothly.

The trouble began a couple of days later when I returned to get my medical clearance signed. I was told there was a problem with my test results. The liver function test had revealed that my liver was damaged. The doctor didn't need to explain what this meant, but she did anyway. She told me that there were a few possible causes for this type of liver damage, with the most common being alcohol abuse. I admitted that I had being partying pretty hard recently, but she informed me that the damage couldn't possibly be attributed to any recent overindulgence, and could only have been caused by long-term alcohol abuse. She urged me to see a liver specialist as soon as possible to establish how serious the damage was. I asked her about my trip to Saudi, and she told me that my priority should be my liver and that she wouldn't be able to give me medical clearance. I pleaded with her, telling her how badly I needed the job, and how I intended to stay off alcohol in Saudi because it was illegal there anyway.

She refused to give in, however, and it was clear that she had reservations about my commitment to staying sober. After all, the extent of my alcohol problem would have been obvious to her from my test results, but I continued to plead with her until eventually she said she would redo the liver test in a few days, and if my results showed an improvement, she would sign the form. Nevertheless, she said she would need to highlight my poor liver function on the report. I doubted if the hospital in Saudi would employ somebody with a dodgy liver. Furthermore, considering that my alcohol binge had continued steadily since my return to Ireland, I sincerely doubted whether the next test would show any improvement.

I can recall that day as if it were yesterday and I was utterly distraught leaving the doctor's office. All my plans were ruined. Even worse, I was probably going to die soon, after a life spent destroying my liver. Being a nurse I'd seen people die from liver disease first hand. It was a horrible way to go. How could I have allowed it to happen to me? I was full of remorse and fear. I had once looked forward to death, in the midst of my terrible depressions, but now it terrified me. I was only 31 years old and my life was over because I'd spent it trying to avoid living. In a way I'd gotten exactly what I'd been after and I had nobody to blame but myself. I coped with this the only way I knew how, and went for a drink.

There was a bar directly across the road from the doctor's office and I spent the next few hours trying to come to terms with the bomb that had just been dropped on me. I looked around the lounge bar at all the other afternoon boozers, and considered the possibility that in a couple of years, or months, I might no longer be a part of any of this—I might be dead. My thoughts swung between this fear and the dread about my plans for the immediate future. I couldn't get to grips with all these black thoughts racing through my head, but I knew I couldn't handle having to stay in Ireland just to get sick and wait to die. That would be unbearable, but then again, I'd been there before and I'd managed to survive.

I left the bar and bought a few cans of cider to drink at home, these were going to be my last drinks, or so I promised myself. I would give up alcohol after this. It was too little too late, but I was determined not to damage my liver any further. I promised any god that might be listening that I would stop for good if there was a way to escape death by liver failure. I knew that psychologists called my behaviour 'bargaining' and that it's a normal reaction to bad news like this. As a nurse I'd seen many patients go through the same thing. I knew that employing this defence mechanism would not change what was happening to me; I had damaged my liver and now I would have to pay the price.

I did manage to stop drinking for the next few weeks, however, and when I went back for my medical the test results were still bad but the doctor agreed to sign my medical form, on the strict condition that I went to see a liver specialist. I didn't feel too hopeful ringing the nursing recruitment agency, but to my surprise, they agreed to let me go to Saudi as planned, probably because they didn't want to lose the money they had already invested in my recruitment.

I ARRIVED IN Riyadh and quickly forgot my promise to seek out a liver specialist. I managed to stay dry for a few weeks, but fear could only deter me from drinking for so long. It turned out I had been mistaken to think that the tough prohibition laws forbidding the sale of alcohol in Saudi would protect me from temptation. Alcohol may have been illegal in the country, but there was a plentiful supply of it, and its illicit nature only made it more tempting to people like me. Upon my arrival at the villa I was staying in, one of the first things shown to me was an improvised still made from dustbin buckets, in which my housemates made alcohol. It turned out that most of the foreigners brewed their own booze and while I was initially a bit tentative about the idea, I soon embraced it. There was always a plentiful supply of cheap, and very strong, hooch knocking about the place and, if anything, I began to drink even more in Saudi than I had before.

As the weeks went by it became easier to downplay the news of my liver damage and the alcoholic's old friend 'denial' began to work its magic on me. I got into a fight on my first night back on the grog, or more accurately, someone took a dislike to me and punched me to the ground. Others said that it wasn't my fault, but nothing like this had ever happened to me when I was sober. The home-made alcohol in Saudi was strong stuff, but I knocked it back like apple juice. On my days off, I went on drinking binges, followed by dry work-days full of remorse and fear about my liver. I continued to make futile promises about how I would change, after the next session, and the session after that. My whole existence was pathetic.

However, I wasn't the only drunk to arrive in Saudi in the hope of finding an escape from alcohol. Another nurse that I met had arrived in the country a few months before me, and he had drank himself to death. In fact, he drowned in his own blood. His liver failure caused portal-hypertension and the blood vessels in his oesophagus burst; it was a horrific way to die. I became certain that I would suffer the same dismal fate if I continued drinking for much longer. I was now running out of ideas.

During a holiday to Vietnam I decided not to return to Saudi. Living there had been an experience, but not one that I wished to continue. It sometimes felt like I was living in a prison. The hospital had taken my passport from me as soon as I had arrived and this really bugged me. The Saudi religious police, the Mattawa, also seemed to have it in for me because every time they saw me in town they questioned me. I had heard horror stories about harassment suffered at the hands of these fanatics, and it scared me shitless. Stories abounded about how they could just take a dislike to you and have you imprisoned for no reason, or even whipped in public. I knew I was going to drink myself to death but, at very least, I wanted to do it somewhere more pleasant than Saudi.

CHAPTER 16

AFTER MY TRIP to Vietnam I ended up on the Thai island of Koh Chang. I still had some money left from Saudi so decided to just devote myself to some hammock-time, I had planned for my finances to keep me going for a year, but this had been overly optimistic of me and I was fast pissing it all down the toilet. The war in Iraq was kicking off, and I spent the days in bars watching the military build-up on TV. I congratulated myself on a good decision not to return to the Middle East. The problem was that I had no idea what to do next.

I weighed up the pros and cons of a return to England or Ireland, and as neither option held much appeal, I decided to just stay on in Thailand and not worry about the future too much. Being drunk most of the time meant that my money was almost all spent after a few months, and I started living on my credit card. An English girl introduced me to English Language teaching, so I decided to give it a try. Teaching work turned out to be easy to find in Bangkok, even though I had none of the necessary qualifications.

Things have changed in recent years, but then, any white face could get a job teaching English in Thailand. The English girl who gave me the idea in the first place taught her own unique grammar structure and vocabulary, and she admitted that she hadn't got a clue what she was doing.

When I now think about the lack of preparation with which I approached my first lesson, I shudder. I didn't know what I was doing. 'Keep the students entertained' was the advice from other drunks in the bars who had been doing it for years. I arrived to my first class with a terrible hangover and no idea about what I was meant to do. My first teaching experience was to a class of 50 secondary school students in a government school in a run-down area of Bangkok. I felt sorry for the students, but much sorrier for myself.

My head was thumping as I entered the classroom, and I was not at all prepared for the volume of noise that hit me. The students were out of control, each one of them shouting or banging something. I was petrified. Some of them looked at me expectantly while the rest just ignored me. I felt sure that they could sense my fear and I knew that this was the worst thing that could happen. I had to somehow gain control of this wild bunch, or they would turn on me, and who knew what could happen then? I considered running away, as was my usual solution to any problem, but there was a Thai teacher standing right in front of the only exit. It felt like he was reading my mind and had anticipated my escape. I remembered what little brats my friends and I had been with new teachers back in my schooldays, and silently prayed that karma wasn't going to give me some pay-back.

I stood frozen in front of the students for a couple of seconds. When I entered the room they had all stood up and a wall of sound hit me: 'Good morning, teacher'. They stood looking at me impatiently. I was saved by the Thai teacher who told them they could sit down. I grabbed one of their textbooks and opened a random chapter about occupations. I selected different students and grilled them about what they wanted to do when they finished school. Some of them didn't have any idea what I was on about, and more of them just didn't have any interest. Thankfully, one or two offered a response: 'policeman', 'soldier' and 'business woman'. I wrote these on the board. One student said 'rice farmer' and everyone laughed. The tension in the class seemed to ease. The next 50 minutes seemed like an eternity, but somehow I muddled through. When class was finished, it was obvious to me that I hadn't got a notion of what I was doing, and I decided that that was to be the end of my teaching career.

I told the agency representative that I had had enough and didn't want to teach any more classes, but either because she didn't understand me, or perhaps because she knew exactly what I was saying, she led me to another classroom full of unruly kids and left abruptly. This next class did go a bit more smoothly, but it would be a while before I felt in any way at ease in front of a group of students. After making it to the end of the first day, I decided to stick it out for the rest of the week, and before I knew it, I had been teaching there for months.

THAILAND SEEMED SO exotic to me in those early days. All the women were so beautiful, I could never remember seeing an unattractive Thai woman. It is easy to understand why people develop such a warped image of Thailand. Most of us only visit certain areas and base our opinion of the entire country on the minority. I suppose it's a bit like visiting Disneyland in Florida and judging the whole of the United States on the theme park. But there is so much more to Thailand than what is seen in the tourist traps.

I would have never thought of myself as being in anyway prudish prior to coming to Thailand. After all, I had slept with many women as a result of drunken one-night-stands—I once tried to calculate the number of women I had slept with over the years but gave up after a hundred. But I did feel uneasy around pornography and prostitution. In my mind, anybody who paid for sex was a degenerate or some type of sex maniac. I hated the idea of paying for sex, and I worried about the health risks associated with it.

My drinking remained out of control during this time. I was now living with *Tep*, a Cambodian girl who I had met on Koh Chang. We fought all the time. The more we argued, the more I drank, and the more I drank, the more we argued. Drinking buddies warned me off her, but I just put this down to jealousy. There was a lot of prostitution on Koh Chang, but I didn't believe that *Tep* was involved in it. She didn't charge me for sex, but after staying with her for a while I learned that she made her money by romancing men over the Internet. These men regularly sent her money and she made a good living this way. I reacted badly when I found out about it, and she couldn't see what my problem was. She said that she needed to support her family, and that I should have been happy that she stayed with me even though I had no money. It was difficult for me to accept this kind of behaviour because it was so different to what I was used to, but I soon learned that this kind of activity was quite acceptable in Thailand and was simply a part of the culture.

At the time, however, I didn't want to be involved with a woman who thought nothing of fleecing someone who felt sorry for her. I knew that I needed to leave her, but just couldn't bring myself to do it. She promised to stop, but after a few days it was obvious that she hadn't. She let her email password slip one day and to my shame I checked her email account. Actually seeing the messages was quite shocking. I had been trying to put some restraints on my alcohol intake because of my teaching commitments, but now I just thought 'fuck it'. I quit teaching, and didn't draw a sober breath for two weeks. In many ways she presented the excuse I needed to go on a spree. In spite of it all I stayed with *Tep* for a while longer. The alcohol numbed my brain and I stopped caring about anything. I am ashamed to admit it but I came the closest I ever have to striking a woman one weekend during this period, but I knew that if I hit *Tep*, it would take my self-loathing to a whole new low, there would be no coming back from that. I truly believed that if things were to continue between us, one of us would end up dead. I had to get away.

I had to bite the bullet and go back to Dublin. I needed to get away from *Tep*, and begin paying off my debts. Drinking buddies told me that I should just default on my debts. Some of these barflies told me how they owed hundreds of thousands back in their home countries, and had no intention of ever paying it back. I just couldn't live like that. I didn't want to be looking over my shoulder for the rest of my life. I wanted to live in Thailand without burning any bridges at home so I decided to return to Ireland and sort my finances out.

Registering as a nurse in Ireland turned out to be more straightforward than I'd thought, and I was soon working five or six nights a week. The wages were good too, and I managed to pay off all my debts in just two months. After three months, I had earned enough money to go back to Thailand.

CHAPTER 17

BACK IN THAILAND, I travelled alone from town to town without seeing much of anywhere except the bars. I'd sometimes get the urge to visit a Buddhist temple after a belly full of beer, and then feel ashamed of myself for turning up drunk. I'd join a drinking crowd for a few days, which provided welcome company, but it was mostly a lonely time. I spent most evenings alone in cheap dingy hotel rooms drinking lager takeouts. I was so lonely that I even started to miss *Tep* and all that drama. I was now mentally defunct. The more I thought about it the more I realised I had returned to Thailand to die. I was sinking further and further into depression, and could no longer blame it on my gloomy surroundings. Here I was in a tropical paradise, and I felt even more depressed than I had before. I was in the depths of despair, and decided once again to seek help for my alcohol problem. This time, however, there would be no addiction treatment centre.

Meditation still intrigued me, and I felt certain that a solution to my alcohol problem would be found through practising it. I remembered how strong my mind had been during my teenage years when meditation was a part of my daily life. If I could take meditation seriously again, perhaps I would be able to gain enough control over my mind to stop drinking for good.

THE 'FOREST MONKS' are a well-known group of meditators in Thailand, but it is hard to find genuine ascetics these days. Most of these wandering monks now live in monasteries. In the past, these Buddhists took their spirituality very seriously and would spend months living alone in the Thai jungle. They devoted most of this time to meditation and learning to deal with their fear of tigers and snakes. Fear of ghosts was quite common, and they overcame this by sleeping in charnel grounds where people buried their dead. One of the most famous monks was Ajahn Mun, whose student Ajahn Chah did much to introduce meditation to the West.

As incredible as it sounds, and even while I was busy drinking myself into oblivion, I had long been harbouring a desire to become a forest monk. This fantasy stayed with me during all those years wasted being drunk. It seemed like a great way to escape my tortured mind. I took some solace in reflecting on the story of Luang Por Teean. He was a layman with a family who made great progress in meditation late in life. It is believed by many that he reached the level of *arahant*—an enlightened one. He waited until his family was grown before he committed himself to intensive training. Eventually, he ordained as a monk. Luang Por Teean's story gave me hope that maybe it wasn't too late for me. After a life devoted to self-absorbed addiction, I hoped that perhaps I could still turn things around.

Wat Rampoeng, situated in Chiang Mai, offered a 26 day meditation retreat. It had a reputation for being hardcore and sounded like it was exactly what I needed. In my drunken mind, I wanted to throw myself into this lifestyle full throttle, and leave my life of alcoholism behind. The meditation techniques taught in Wat Rampoeng were believed to be an effective way to reach enlightenment. At the time, I would have been ecstatic if they could just help me to get and remain sober—enlightenment was far too ambitious a goal for me. The temple's Mahasi method practised walking meditation as well as sitting meditation. A lot of my problem with meditation in the past—during my brief periods of sobriety—was that I was too full of energy to maintain the stillness required. For this reason, meditating while moving really appealed to me.

The day of the retreat was fast approaching and I began to doubt whether I could go through with it. I needed to quit alcohol a couple of days before the retreat began, as I knew that turning up at the temple smelling of drink or in the middle of withdrawals wouldn't be acceptable. My last session prior to the temple had been the most enjoyable in ages, and I really struggled with the temptation to drink after it. Withdrawal hadn't been too bad this time, but I began to see the retreat as just another ridiculous notion of mine. Something inside me must have been urging me to go through with it, however, as I somehow managed to stay sober and arrive at the temple on the arranged day.

THE FIRST DAY of the retreat wasn't too intense. I spent the morning learning the Mahasi meditation method with another group of newcomers. We were expected to follow one hour of walking meditation with one hour of sitting meditation and repeat. As the days went by, we were expected to increase the number of sets performed. On the first day, we were only expected to meditate for eight hours. I immediately took to the walking meditation. It involved moving very slowly, observing mentally every movement in a step: rising, lifting, moving, lowering, touching and putting. My concentration levels increased as I continued to observe all of these steps, and this helped with my sitting meditation. The monk had compared the walking meditation to charging a battery. He explained how this power could be put to use later in more formal meditation.

By the third day I was meditating for up to ten hours. The meditation practice and the tranquillity of the temple meant that I experienced a previously unknown sense of peace. My worries about addiction melted away, and life took on a simple rhythm. Most of the day was spent in complete silence as talking was discouraged at the temple. Any type of entertainment was forbidden—we weren't even allowed to read books about Buddhism or meditation. Our only focus was the practice of meditation, and the only interruption to this was our morning meal and a daily chat with the head monk.

Temple life began at 4am and I would begin meditating for the day at that time. At 6am the bell would ring for breakfast, and as it would now have been 16 hours since the last meal, I'd be hungry. We were expected to follow some of the monk's rules, and one of these was that no food was to be taken between midday and dawn the next day. This wasn't just deprivation for the sake of it, but was in keeping with the belief that it is easier to meditate on an empty stomach. Our entire day was devoted to meditation, with just a few breaks allowed for showering, washing our white 'uniforms', and daily visits to the Ajahn Suphan to report on our experiences.

At the end of the retreat we were expected to attempt a 'determination'. This is a three day period when you are expected to meditate around the clock, not even stopping to sleep. The bed was removed from my *kuti* and the only time I was allowed to leave my room was for ten minutes to report to Ajahn Suphan. On my way to this meeting I had to wear a sign around my neck which informed people that I was doing a determination and, therefore, they shouldn't speak to me. Meals were placed outside my *kuti* each morning.

During these 72 hours, time stopped having any real meaning. There wasn't much to mark the passing of the days so I just gave in completely to the practice: walking meditation followed by sitting meditation, hour after hour. It wasn't called a determination for nothing and it took a lot of willpower to keep going, especially during the night when fighting tiredness became a real struggle.

I had expected some sort of amazing insight to occur at the end of the determination, but that wasn't how it worked. Sometimes during the 72 hours my perceptions would change and the world would appear less threatening. I felt truly peaceful. In the final hour of the determination I felt tantalisingly close to the spiritual experience that I had encountered on the bus in London, but like trying to remember a dream, the more I tried to grasp it, the further it slipped away.

I left Wat Rampoeng fully at ease with the world and with my place in it. It did feel as though something had changed inside me, and I realised that this peaceful state was only a glimpse into how things could be. The feeling did last a few days and probably would have lasted longer if I hadn't returned to alcohol. My brief taste of a clear mind only made the mental torture of being back in the midst of addiction all the more painful. I could see just how good things could be, but frustratingly, I could not recreate the experience of peace outside the temple. After a few weeks I did attempt to go back to Wat Rampoeng to regain the mental clarity that I had lost, but this time it was harder to take a break from my addiction. I dreamt of becoming a monk at the temple and spending the rest of my days at peace. I just couldn't get through more than a couple of days sober and I knew I couldn't return to the temple. I kept trying, but mostly it felt like I was fighting a losing battle.

DURING ONE OF these attempts to detox before returning to the temple, I met a girl called Oa in Chiang Mai. It was my second day sober, and I was sitting outside a restaurant, reading a book and sipping on a soda water, trying to avoid the bars. Oa came over to my table and we fell into an easy conversation. I was not looking for any sort of romantic relationship, especially not another inter-cultural one, but I was glad of the chance to practice speaking some Thai, and of the temporary respite from my now constant feeling of loneliness.

Oa was attractive in an unadorned way. Her clothes were worn for comfort and not purely decoration, but they looked good on her. She seemed happy in her own skin which was a quality that I always admired in others. She laughed easily, and seemed interested in what I had to say.

I enjoyed talking with Oa so much that we ended up meeting again the next day. Within a few weeks we were a couple. On one of our dates I decided to have a few beers and it was business as usual in regards to my drinking. Thoughts of entering the temple for another meditation retreat were put on hold, indefinitely.

My reservations about entering into another inter-cultural relationship turned out to be completely unfounded. Oa was nothing like *Tep*: she didn't like to argue, and never shouted, there was no string of boyfriends sending her money, and she expressed no dreams of becoming rich. She did want to start a family one day, and her dream place to live was the village where she had lived most of her life. In some ways her goals in life seem limited to me, but the more I got to know her the more they made sense. I began to see that the simple life had a lot going for it and that accumulating things and experiences was not necessarily the path to happiness—it just meant an endless hunger. I knew from experience that the more I had, the more I wanted and needed.

We stayed in a few different places in Thailand before moving to Oa's village. Like my other girlfriends before her, and as I myself had so often believed, Oa naively thought that a change of scenery might temper my drinking. Nevertheless, I didn't volunteer any information that would have set her misconception straight. We moved to Chat Trakan which was 120km from the nearest city. There were no bars in the local vicinity, but I still managed to spend each day getting drunk. My living room became my bar, and it never closed. Pub crawls were replaced by motorbike rides around the Thai countryside, searching for restaurants and bars where I could stock up on cans of Chang lager.

Oa was keen to start a family, but I made it clear that this wasn't going to happen. It wasn't that I didn't want children, a big part of me did, but I knew that there was no way I could take responsibility for a baby. It made me sad to think I might never have a family, but a drunk becoming a father is a terrible thing and I knew it. I had done a lot of bad things in my life but this was one action that I wasn't prepared to be responsible for. Oa accepted my decision, but I could tell it was difficult for her.

We lived in a white, one-bedroom house in Chat Trakan, on the edge of the village, which had a big garden with all types of exotic fruit growing. Being situated right next to a large paddy field meant that the house was often invaded by all types of insects, snakes, and rats. I was horrified by all this when I first moved to the village, and slept with a large knife by the bed. After a year, however, having a scorpion or a snake stare at me during a midnight call of nature no longer fazed me.

My life sounded exciting and glamorous to friends, but in reality it rarely felt this way to me. Ostensibly, I was living an idyllic life in peaceful surroundings, but privately, I was in turmoil. I was trapped in a cycle of drinking, wanting to stop, yet drinking even more. I suffered from almost constant abdominal pain and for almost four years I didn't have a solid bowel movement. I got no pleasure from alcohol anymore but was powerless to stop drinking. How my day was going to turn out was decided by my ability to ingest alcohol. Being able to hold the alcohol down meant a bearable day, but if I couldn't, it meant a day lying around shaking and waiting for my stomach to settle. My life was completely pointless.

I was carving out a reputation for myself as the village drunk. People commented on the amount of beer bottles that accumulated around our house—a Thai village keeps no secrets. There were a few other drunks in the area, but being a foreigner, I really stood out. I was still relatively young too, which made me all the more gossip-worthy. The other winos were old guys who had worked hard all their lives.

Occasionally I would manage to get through a week or two of withdrawals and stay sober for a while. I'd return to some form of meditative practice during these breaks, and I remained convinced that the solution to my addiction lay in this contemplative life. The problem was that this path wasn't an easy one to follow, at least not for me, and as soon as it got a bit tough I'd give it up. I had learned during my teenage years, however, that it was by continuing with meditation when it seemed the most difficult, that you came out the other side feeling stronger, but years of addiction meant I had little patience for periods of stagnation. My failure to persist with meditation meant that I missed out on many of the benefits I could have received.

I trawled the Internet nightly in an attempt to find a solution to my problem. I was crying out for help, of any kind, but was getting none. At this stage, I felt I'd read all the information there was to read about recovery, and it just left me feeling cynical and angry. I joined an online AA meeting but soon became irritated with the broken-record comments about needing to attend regular live meetings. I explained to them that my home was over 400km from the nearest AA meeting, but they still insisted that I make the effort to get to them. It was so unreasonable as to be absurd and the AA message of 'our way or no way' irritated me so much that I eventually stopped using their web forums.

I still believe AA is a great programme, and I have seen it work for many people, but it was no longer working for me. I knew that if I was ever to escape from my addiction, I would want it permanently out of my life, but AA's intent seemed to me to be to focus on the fact that alcoholics could never escape their addiction: 'Once an alcoholic, always an alcoholic'. That wasn't what I wanted for myself. If I was going to have to spend my life focusing on alcohol then I figured I may as well just drink the stuff. What I wanted was to get away from it completely.

CHAPTER 18

I HAD MORE or less given up all hope of recovery, and believed that my death from liver failure was inevitable, when I came across a website for Wat Thamkrabok. I had been living in Thailand for a few years by now and wondered why I hadn't heard of this Buddhist temple before. A soft voice in my head suggested that perhaps it was a case of 'the student being ready and the teacher appearing'. After looking through the information on the website I felt hopeful for the first time in a long time. The more I read, the more I was convinced that this could work for me.

I tried to share my enthusiasm about Thamkrabok with Oa, but was disappointed when she appeared cautious. She had every right to treat any of my plans with suspicion—I had frequently promised to change my ways, and she had heard it all before. I never followed through on any of my drunken schemes, so why should this time be any different?

Oa already knew about the temple, and apparently it was well known and respected in Thailand. When I asked her why she hadn't mentioned it to me before, she explained that if you returned to your addiction after getting treatment in the temple, terrible things would happen. She clearly wasn't too confident about my ability to stop. She'd heard stories of people relapsing after leaving the temple and soon ending up dead. I found the tales hard to believe, but mocking the beliefs of the local people was one of the few things that really annoyed Oa. There were many things which Oa accepted as fact which I would previously have considered nonsensical or even foolish, but now I tried to approach these beliefs with an open mind—albeit a sometimes openly doubtful mind

The next morning my enthusiasm hadn't waned, and I decided that nothing could be gained by delaying my departure. I needed to go before this delicate motivation ebbed away. This unexpected last chance needed to be grasped immediately. Oa was warming up to the idea, but my drinking at 6am created fresh doubt in her mind. I explained to her that these last few beers were necessary in order to delay any withdrawal symptoms until I was safely tucked up in the temple. I pleaded with Oa to ring Thamkrabok and ask if they would accept me as soon as possible.

On the phone, they informed Oa that there would be no problem with me just coming and checking myself in straight away. There was no application process and so long as they had a bed for me I could stay. They had a space available now, and I would be welcome to admit myself. They agreed that it would be best that I come as soon as possible before changing my mind—we addicts can be such a fickle bunch.

I wanted to get to the temple without delay, but my current tourist visa was just about to expire. To renew it I would have to leave the country then come back in again, not a particularly difficult process, just an inconvenient one. The nearest border was Burma and this was a frequent destination for my visa-runs. I could get to Mae Rim and back in one day on my motorbike.

I decided to go straight to the temple once my new visa was obtained. It would involve covering a great distance, but I frequently made long journeys on my Honda Wave, a reliable if not overly powerful bike. I always enjoyed the opportunity to really think things over on these long trips, and saw this as a chance to psych myself up for a complete recovery. On the other hand, I was aware that I risked talking myself out of it and ending up going on a bender.

I told Oa about my plan and she looked at me disapprovingly. She had seen me knock back a couple of bottles of Singha beer for breakfast, and I knew her views about my riding my bike while intoxicated. I disapproved of it myself, but that didn't stop me doing it almost every day. Rationally, I knew that riding a motorbike while drunk was extremely dangerous, but for me, it felt so much safer. I'd rarely been sober when learning to ride a motorbike in Thailand so it just felt natural to ride this way.

The fact I now had another chance to defeat my addiction meant that a farewell drink felt reasonable. I would allow myself to indulge one last time, and I would risk riding my motorbike inebriated one final time. It wasn't that I expected to get any enjoyment from these drinks. I wouldn't. It was just that the idea of travelling somewhere in the midst of withdrawals felt dangerous, and the constant craving for alcohol would make the whole experience torturous. I just needed alcohol to function, at least until safely on the other side of the withdrawal process.

I said my farewells to Oa and to my dog Cola, and I promised them both that the next time they saw me I would be a new man. Logically I knew there was no reason for this time to be any different than all my previous attempts to quit alcohol, but something inside me felt different and I was optimistic about this new Buddhist approach. Unfortunately, however, with my history of relapse there could be no guarantees.

Thamkrabok would only offer me one chance to get sober—the website made it clear that you only got one chance to attend, and that was fine by me. I knew this was my last chance anyway. I doubted my liver would last much longer, and the constant fight to gain control over myself had worn me down. The idea of continuing the fight seemed impossible, and I didn't have the energy anymore. I made a promise to myself: this would be my last attempt at quitting. If Thamkrabok failed then there would be no more attempts to control my addiction. I would just give in to it and continue drinking until it killed me.

I MANAGED TO travel for two hours before feeling the need to stop for a drink. I had reached Sukothai and knew from previous stays that there were a few guest-houses with restaurants which catered for westerners. I liked to eat western food when given a chance, and as these places were used to having people drinking at all times of the day and night, I felt less self-conscious about drinking there during the day.

My delicate stomach had no desire for any food, but I hadn't eaten much in the last few days and I knew that a failure to get food inside me would soon have consequences. I needed the energy to get to the temple the next day. I reasoned that once I had another couple of beers my stomach would be more appreciative of solids.

I went into a bar and bought a Singha beer but my stomach was acting up. I swallowed a mouthful but instantly felt like vomiting it back up and struggled to keep the drink in my mouth. I hoped that nobody noticed my retching motions. I slowly eased the alcohol back down my throat. This time it stayed down and by the time I had half-finished the bottle my stomach had started to settle again.

After a few more bottles I felt ready to get on the road again. The last leg of the journey was through the mountains. The few drinks had aroused a craving for more and it was a real struggle to keep going. I fought a private battle each time I approached a garage or a shop, but I promised myself that I wouldn't stop again until my petrol tank needed filling. I kept my mind busy by planning my final night on the sauce in Mae Sot. I would get good and drunk one final time.

I eventually made it through my tank of petrol and allowed myself another drink. I bought a couple of cans of Chang and sat down on a bench at the side of the shop, and began swallowing. Halfway through the first can, I threw up. I knew I wouldn't be able to get any more drink inside me for a while. It was infuriating— my stomach was rejecting the stuff my mind was really craving. I continued on my journey to Mae Sot. My stomach hurt terribly and the pain was spreading to the rest of my abdomen. It was a pain I always associated with my liver declaring it just wasn't happy.

I was still feeling sick when I arrived at my destination, and I felt bitter and sorry for myself. My last night of drinking was going to be spent shivering and shaking in a strange hotel room. I felt I deserved this final time with my old friend—drink. Tomorrow I would be ready to face the discomfort of alcohol leaving my system, but not now. I wanted an opportunity to say goodbye to alcohol with a bang. I could well remember the claims in AA that if you couldn't remember your last drink then you hadn't had it yet. I was determined to make my last drinks memorable, but my stomach was getting in the way. I bought a few bottles of beer in the hope that the next hour or two would be spent slowly sipping these, and that this would settle my stomach enough to allow me a final night on the town. It wasn't to be, however. I barely managed to drink half a bottle during the rest of the night because my stomach was in such turmoil, but, somehow, I eventually managed to fall asleep.

CHAPTER 19

I WOKE UP after a restless night, aching for alcohol. My attempts to drink at 6am were as futile as the night before. I tried to finish an almost full bottle which I had opened prior to falling to sleep. I thought the stale lager would be easier to ingest, but I only managed to swallow a few mouthfuls before I puked it all back up. I spent the next hour lying in bed looking at the half-full bottle, which seemed to be mocking me. The drug the rest of my body was crying out for just couldn't get past my stomach. There was no point in wasting any more time in the hotel. I wasn't sure what time the border to Burma opened, but decided to make my way there anyway.

The border turned out to be just a 15-minute-ride away from the hotel. I arrived at Mae Rim where the Thai border with Burma is located. Mae Rim is a fairly lacklustre place, which also seems to be a little shady. I imagined most of the people around there and in the border town of Chiang Rai were gangsters or smugglers.

It was necessary to cross a bridge to reach the Burmese side of the border. This no-man's-land was filled with a variety of people who seemed to have turned this area into their business location. A typical sight is the Burmese entrepreneur, i.e. a man who strikes up a conversation with foreigners crossing the border and accompanies them to the other side chatting all the way. He will point out the building you need, and then expect to get paid for this unnecessary service. I was in no mood for this would-be tycoon and his company today, and legged it over the bridge as fast as my sick body could carry me.

Foreigners in Thailand call these trips to renew our visas 'visa runs', and I needed to make this trip every few months. I had always used this as an excuse for hitting the drink particularly hard. My favourite trip would be to Vientiane in Laos, which I would turn into a three day holiday, sometimes even longer, but my declining health and wealth meant that these trips were no longer possible.

The Burmese side of the border is a lot different from the Thai side. The stark difference in wealth between the two countries always hits me immediately. Mae Rim is far from a glamorous area, but when compared to the opposite Burmese town, it appears opulent.

The border guards on the Burmese side of the divide must be the friendliest in the world. They always seem happy to see me and offer warm smiles when taking my passport. Obtaining the visa for Burma involves a bit of paperwork but the guards are keen to make the wait as pleasant as possible. They allow you to sit in their office and provide a chair along with offers of ice water. Once the stamp was out of the way, I headed straight across the bridge and back to the Thai side.

The good thing about so few westerners using this particular border meant that there was usually no queuing up to get a visa. The bad thing was that Thai immigration had plenty of time to give each passport a proper inspection. I was always very nervous waiting for the stamp, dreading that they might refuse me.

The flipping of the pages back and forth went on forever and I was beginning to feel nauseous. My hand was shaking while I filled out the entry form, and I'm sure the officer had a fairly good idea why this was. The longer she inspected my passport, the more I began to feel dirty and like a bit of a low-life. I wondered whether I would admit someone like me into my country if I were in her position, but then I figured it was better not to think too much about it. She asked me how I was supporting myself in Thailand, the unspoken insinuation being that I was working illegally. I tried to assure her that I was surviving on money from outside the country, and although she looked at me sceptically, she stamped my passport with the precious entry visa. I tried not to look too relieved as I took my passport from her and walked back to my bike.

CHAPTER 20

I WAS NOW free to make my way to the temple. It was just after 8am and I wanted to get there before 4pm. I still hadn't given up hope of having some last drinks before admitting myself. In fact the closer I got to Thamkrabok the more intense this craving became. My stomach was still in a heap and so I remained in the miserable state of needing alcohol, but not being able to ingest it. As the withdrawal symptoms intensified and coursed through my body, I began to feel tense and was on the verge of having a panic attack.

As noon approached I began to give up hope of any farewell drinks. I considered delaying my arrival at the temple by a day and my alcohol-starved mind latched onto this idea with a massive sense of relief. One more night, to say goodbye to an old friend who had been such an important part of my life. I wanted my final drink to be bittersweet, to part with alcohol on good terms. Despite all the suffering I had endured because of alcohol, it had once been a good friend and strong ally in my times of need, or so I led myself to believe.

Lopburi was a city near the temple where I considered spending the night. I could sleep for a few hours and then hopefully wake up raring to go. I had passed through Lopburi a few times on the train and had always been interested in staying there. I could have a few drinks that night and arrive at the temple nice and early in the morning. Why not? One more night wasn't going to do much harm, was it? In the end though, sanity prevailed. There might not be a tomorrow for me. If I stayed in Lopburi I could end up on a bender with all thoughts of treatment forgotten. It also irritated me to think that Oa probably believed this was what I was up to on this journey, even though the truth was I was now very close to doing that very thing.

As a means of renewing my determination I focused on the reasons why I wanted to stay sober. The obvious reason was that I didn't want to die. But maybe death was the only way to escape addiction? What if death wasn't even the end of it? What if it was only one life out of many and I was destined to live this useless existence over and over again? I had learned during my two previous years of sobriety that life had a habit of throwing lessons at us until we learned from them, so maybe this process continued even after death. I desperately wanted to get beyond addiction in this life.

Another reason for wanting to quit was that there was just absolutely no enjoyment in it anymore, none whatsoever. There hadn't been in years. I kept on thinking that maybe the good times would return, but

I knew in my heart this was just a futile hope.

I passed through Lopburi without stopping. As I guided my motorbike through the old part of the city I saw troops of monkeys, which the city is renowned for. I had another 30km to go from there, and I arrived at the temple just before 4pm.

I rode around the temple grounds for some time, trying to locate the admissions office. I passed many buildings that seemed vacant and in the process of decay. I worried I had perhaps arrived in the wrong place. I passed an immense stone structure which was comprised of giant Buddhas sitting around in a circle. I had no idea where I was going, and no idea what the admissions office looked like. I did another full circle of the temple and felt sure I had passed everywhere in the temple grounds before finally looking for help.

I stopped at an empty restaurant, decorated in the typical minimalist Thai style. I could hear someone working near the back of the restaurant so I made my way there, and found a woman chopping meat. She was startled by my sudden appearance, but her expression soon relaxed into a familiar Thai smile. She grabbed my hand and pulled me towards the front of the restaurant where she pointed out a building and now that I looked more carefully it did seem to be an office—I had ridden past it twice.

I made the short journey to the office by foot. It was a relief to stretch my legs after being on the motorbike for so long. Initially I thought the office was closed, but then the door opened for me and there were a couple of people inside. A monk tapped away on a keyboard and I made my way over to him. He barely looked up from the computer as I explained why I was there. He motioned to a chair where I presumed he wanted me to wait. The longer I waited, the more worried I became that he had misunderstood my reason for arriving at the temple.

During the previous 30 hours or so I had imagined all types of scenarios about how my arrival at the temple would occur. I had expected fuss and commotion over a westerner turning up at their door to recover from his addiction. I had made the epic decision to face my addiction once and for all, and I hadn't even needed to be dragged there! I had been expecting a big to-do, but my arrival didn't even cause a ripple. I then realised I was just another desperate addict who had arrived at the gates of the temple in the hope of finding some type of liberation. They had seen it all before, and while I might have been playing the leading role in the drama that was my life, this meant nothing to them.

After a few minutes a western monk arrived in the office and invited me to join him at a desk. His name was Phra Hans, and he was originally from Switzerland. His kind face was tranquillity personified. I described my history to him and tried to convey to him my determination to quit the booze, with the help of the temple. He listened without reaction until I had finished my speech.

The Swiss monk eased my troubled mind somewhat when he stated that the temple was indeed a rehab facility, but then deflated it when he added that it could not get me sober. He explained that the temple could detox my body and provide me with tools which would make recovery possible, but the willingness to stay sober had to come from within me; the temple could not supply me with this determination. The real work of recovery had to start and finish with me.

Phra Hans explained Thamkrabok's theory of addiction, which immediately made sense to me. There was no talk of disease or an alcoholic gene. Instead, the monk explained how my addiction had been a tool which I had been using to cope with life. For a while this tool had been somewhat useful—if it hadn't been, then I wouldn't have used it. Alcohol had helped me to cope with anxiety and the frustrations of life in the beginning. The problem was the tool that I had been employing to cope with life had stopped working, but I had failed to abandon it. Phra Hans went on to explain that the reason why many of these negative feelings had arisen in the first place was because I had lost my path in life. If I could find my way back to this path, then there would no longer be a need for me to employ an external tool to help me cope with life. There would no longer be a need for any addiction.

The Swiss monk's speech sounded very logical to me, but as the alcohol had by now left my system, I was finding it hard to concentrate fully. I was feeling shaky and my whole body felt uncomfortable. I wanted to roll into a ball somewhere and just wait it out. The truth of the monk's words resonated with me, however, and I felt sure their importance would become an influence on my recovery. But for now, I had to force myself to listen and remain sitting in the hard plastic chair.

Somewhere during our conversation my status changed from 'interested applicant' to 'patient at the temple'. Instead of talking about what the temple could offer if I became a patient, the monk began telling me about what would happen during my stay. I wasn't exactly sure when this approval of my admission had been granted, but it was a relief to know that I had been accepted as a patient of Thamkrabok.

I filled out a few forms with my jittery hands and tried hard not to make a total mess of the job. I had to hand over my passport, money, mobile phone and credit cards, and was told they would be locked away in the temple's safe. Handing my passport over was a struggle for me, as I had sworn never to allow myself to be without it again after Saudi, but if I wanted to stay at the temple then that was the rule I had to obey.

I was escorted behind a curtain where I was joined by two young monks. They checked my bags for contraband and instructed me to remove all my clothes. This was all quite embarrassing and I began to resent the suspicion. I wasn't a junkie or a criminal. I was only a drunk.

The monks gave me a red laundry basket and informed me this would contain all the items I was allowed to take with me into the detox area. Except for underwear I would need to leave all my clothes behind. As well as underpants I only put in my towel, a couple of books, and some toiletries. The monks checked my wash-bag sceptically and they focused on my toothpaste. I had never been to prison but I assume this same procedure would be carried out there.

I was handed two red uniforms, and my feeling of being in prison only increased when I put one on. The uniform was very distinctive and I knew if I were to wear it outside the temple, everyone would easily recognise where I had come from—I suppose that was the point.

Once I had dressed in my new uniform, I picked up my basket of personal belongings and followed the two monks out of the office and down a short path to a fenced-in area. One of the monks called out and a gate was opened from the side. Then they led me into the 'Hay'.

CHAPTER 21

THE 'HAY' IS where the junkies and alcoholics live while they are going through treatment. It is separated from the rest of the temple on one side by iron bars. It is not escape proof, but escape from the temple would be difficult for most westerners to accomplish without their money or passport, while wearing a bright red uniform which marked the wearer out as some type of reprobate.

Inside the gate of the Hay was a table with a group of monks sitting around it. One of them approached me and asked me what was I there for, which stumped me initially. Was this a trick question? I replied 'alcohol' with little confidence. His next question threw me even further: 'How long do you want to quit for?' This time I had to admit my confusion. He clarified the matter by simply repeating the question, and adding that I could promise to stop for one year, five years, ten years, or life. I was now totally convinced that he was trying to trick me and that an incorrect response would have me expelled from the temple. I replied more forcibly than I'd intended to and told him that I wanted to stop for life. He smiled and wrote my response down on a small scrap of paper but this really bothered me. How could he write such vital information on such unofficial looking paper?

The two monks left me inside a small dorm room, which contained three beds and little else. I was given the bed nearest a window that looked out onto the courtyard we had just passed through. There was a door next to the window, which appeared to be locked. On the way to this room we had passed through a larger room with more beds and a few mattresses. There was nobody in either of these rooms, but there were signs of occupation everywhere. The bed next to mine, for instance, had a wash bag and a few personal belongings scattered messily on top of it. These provided few clues as to what type of person their owner might be, however, and I began to worry about who I would be sharing the room with.

I had no idea what I was supposed to do now. The monks said I would be going for my *satja* ceremony later on, but I didn't know what time this was going to be or what I should do until then. This was meant to be the real heart of the treatment, and according to the website, it would be this *satja* that would help keep you sober once you left the temple. The *satja* was a sacred vow—a promise you made to yourself never to touch drugs or alcohol for the period of time you had chosen.

The monks had disappeared, so I couldn't question them any further. I was frustrated with the lack of organisation that had accompanied my admission. I needed to calm down, but had nothing with which to distract myself. I waited on the bed, wanting company, while at the same time feeling nervous about having to meet strangers.

There was a small locker beside my bed, and I used this to store my books. I had only managed to bring two books with me, and I hoped there would be more available in the temple. I hated when I had nothing to read, and it seemed I would have a lot of free time during my stay at the temple. I had a book about Buddhist meditation, and a horror story by Dean Koontz, which I predicted would be easy to read, even if my concentration was poor. It could be difficult to obtain secondhand books living in an isolated part of Thailand like I did, so this meant that any book I got my hands on felt precious. It also meant that I read stuff I would previously not really have considered; the Dean Koontz book fell into this category.

Waiting on the bed gave me a chance to think about my introduction to the temple. It wasn't long before my thoughts began to fixate on the monk's question about the length of time I wanted to quit alcohol for. I realised at this point the question was linked to my *satja* ceremony. I started to doubt my decision to abstain for life, and whether I really had the strength to make that sort of commitment. A familiar opponent reared its ugly head, and told me I would always need alcohol and that my attempts to quit my addiction were futile. I tried my best to ignore this old enemy and to keep these negative thoughts at bay.

The usual method of treating addiction is to view it as a type of disease that is beyond our control, but I had grown to disagree with this way of looking at things. My interest in meditation had helped me to realise that change was possible. If it wasn't, then what would be the point of any of it? If I was responsible for the mess I had made of my life, then surely I had some power to change it around. During my two years of sobriety the feeling that 'my disease' was always close by never quite left me. I didn't want to go back to that. I wanted to take control of my life and take responsibility for my actions. No more excuses.

My thoughts were interrupted by the entrance of a pale-faced man who had the look of a drug user about him. He sat down on the bed next to mine and fiddled around with his locker for a short while before speaking. He introduced himself and, to my great surprise, it turned out that he was also from Dublin. Here I was in a detox facility in Thailand and the person in the next bed was from the same city as me!

Matt had arrived in Thailand earlier that same day. He had come with his partner *Sharon,* accompanied by another Dubliner called *Steve. Steve* was a former patient of the temple who had been so delighted by his recovery that he was now encouraging others to go to the temple. *Matt* and *Sharon* were both addicted to heroin and it had been *Matt*'s idea, supported by *Steve*, to come to the temple.

I was keen to discover what *Matt* thought of Thailand and the temple so far. I was disappointed to find that he spoke negatively about everything; I had never previously met anybody who was anything but ecstatic to be in Thailand, but I suppose *Matt* had arrived in less than ideal circumstances. He said coming to the temple had been a big mistake and that it was a complete dump. *Matt* was shocked to hear I'd been living in Thailand for the previous three and a half years. He said I must be a nut-case. 'Why would anyone want to leave Ireland to come live in a piss-poor sweaty shit-hole like Thailand?' The half-crazed look on *Matt*'s face was enough to discourage me from trying to defend the country which I had come to love.

I listened to *Matt* complain about everything and anything for a while more until he began to roll on the bed and moan loudly. I felt obliged to ask him if he was alright, but then wondered if it was wiser to just ignore him. I asked anyway. He described his withdrawal symptoms to me, the most distressing symptom at present being body cramps. I asked him if there was anything I could do to help him, and he replied by saying that unless I had some heroin on me, there was absolutely nothing I could do to help him.

After a while his symptoms subsided and he was ready for more chat. He told me about his trip to Thailand and how he, *Sharon* and *Steve* had ended up having to stay in Dubai for a night. To my complete astonishment he told me he had tried to score heroin in Dubai. When I expressed my incredulity at his actions, *Matt* shrugged it off as no big deal and didn't seem to have any inkling of the inherent danger involved in his behaviour. The only thing that concerned *Matt* was that he had been forced to enter withdrawals before even arriving at the temple, and he was not at all happy with how badly his trip had been planned.

I told *Matt* I was about to go for my *satja* ceremony, and he told me that he and *Sharon* had already gone through the ceremony earlier. I asked *Matt* to describe it, and all he had to say was that it had been a complete waste of time, and that it had involved sitting uncomfortably in front of a monk while he recited some mumbo jumbo.

At the time I was dealing with my own problems, so I warned myself to keep out of his way as much as possible. I didn't want to get sucked into his negativity. If this was going to be my last chance at recovery, then I didn't need some contrary Irishman bringing me down. I wanted to take the *satja* ceremony seriously. I had learnt from previous experiences that you only ever get out of these things what you are prepared to put in. I pulled my meditation book off the shelf and began leafing through the pages. I couldn't concentrate on any of the words because my thoughts were racing, but it helped me to avoid having to converse any further with *Matt*.

CHAPTER 22

A MONK ARRIVED to take me to the *satja* ceremony a few hours later. His name was Gop, and he had lived in the United States for 12 years. While there, he had developed a taste for drugs and this was the path that led him to Thamkrabok.

He told me some of his story as we walked to the *satja* ceremony. He had actually been tricked into attending the temple. His family in Thailand had heard about his drug addiction and they formulated a plan to get him back to Thailand and into treatment. It is traditional in Thailand for men to ordain as monks for at least a short while in their lives. Many donate the merit accumulated by doing this to female members of the family who can't ordain as monks. Gop's family asked that he ordain as a monk for the sake of his sick grandmother. They put a lot of emotional pressure on him until he eventually returned to Thailand and put on the robes. He didn't realise he would be spending his monkhood in the Hay until the gates were locked behind him. For a while he had been angry with his family for tricking him, but now he just accepted it. He confided in me, however, that he would probably go back on drugs once he left the temple and returned to the States.

We arrived at a *sala*, which is an open air building with just a small roof with pillars to support it. A monk was waiting for us inside. Although monks in Thailand do not wear any symbols to donate rank, it is usually fairly easy to spot the senior ones. It is something about the way they carry themselves. They look comfortable in the robes, unlike the younger monks who remind me of school children wearing their uniform for the first time. The monk before me had the air of somebody very senior.

I wondered if there was still time to change my mind and select a five year time limit for my *satja*. All I could think about was escaping but I would need to make up my mind quickly because once the *satja* was made there would be no going back. Before I had time to decide, however, monk Gop ushered me to kneel beside a Thai man who was also wearing the red uniform. We were both kneeling in front of the senior monk. My withdrawal symptoms had been coming in waves over the last few hours, and I was now shaking violently as the senior monk began to recite Pali chants. I was self-conscious about this until I noted that the Thai man was shaking along with me. Occasionally the monk stopped reciting and asked the two of us to repeat a Pali verse. I mumbled unintelligibly and just waited for the ceremony to be over. My knees began to ache from kneeling for so long, and I felt miserable.

The monk's chants eventually began to wind down, and I was glad to be able to get up off my knees. There was no going back now. I had made the *satja* for life and now that it was done, all my doubts faded away.

As I PASSED through the main room on the way to my dorm, I saw a few other westerners sitting around. Back in my room, *Matt* was still there, wearing a sarong. There had been one on my bed when I'd arrived, but I had no idea why it had been left there. *Matt* told me one of the monks had instructed him to put it on, and had left similar instructions for me. We needed to wear it for the medicine ceremony. Now the reason for the sarong was clear—it was to avoid getting vomit on the red uniform that we wore the rest of the day. The reality of the medicine session began to hit me, and while it had seemed like an interesting idea on the Internet, it now seemed threatening.

The medicine was an emetic and the ingredients are kept as a closely guarded secret. All the herbs in the medicine come from the nearby hills and forests. Apparently the female founder of the temple had come across these ingredients while wandering around the area and had somehow come to the realisation that a certain combination of herbs would help addicts detoxify from their drug. My mind boggled wondering how the founder could possibly have arrived at this idea and how she had discovered this magic combination, but I had to stop this line of questioning in my mind straight away. I knew from experience where this type of thinking would lead—it would lead to doubt, which would lead to mistrust, and eventually back to the misery of addiction.

I hadn't eaten anything all day and wondered how this would affect me when I took the medicine that would cause me to vomit. The monks had told me that I wasn't to eat anything from midday prior to taking the medicine, but no food had touched my stomach for a much longer period than this. I had also been informed that fizzy drinks before the ceremony would make the experience far more unpleasant. These restrictions would be in place for five days while I had to take the medicine.

I didn't think that vomiting could hold any surprises for me. After all, it went hand and hand with drinking and it was something I had been doing regularly for years. The difference was that in the past, this vomiting had been dulled by drunkenness. I had never vomited in a temple before, or openly in front of other people, and being sick was not something I ever willingly induced. The whole idea of the vomiting ceremony seemed a bit wrong somehow, and the enormity of what was about to happen began to dawn on me. I will never forget the events which followed.

An electric bell rang somewhere in the temple, signalling that the medicine ceremony was about to commence. The walk from our dorm to the area where the ceremony was to take place felt like a walk to the gallows. I kept close to *Matt* and we were joined by some other westerners from the other room, who had been through the ritual a few times before. As we passed out of the dorm we were joined by a young pale-faced girl who I rightly guessed to be *Matt*'s other half. We gave each other a smile, but this was no time for chitchat. Those who had been through the ceremony before offered us advice as we walked.

The ceremony would take place in a courtyard near the entrance to the Hay. This area had been vacant when I passed through it earlier, but now it had the appearance of a fairground with the large crowd of spectators that had gathered. A group of Thais had even assembled into a band with improvised instruments. One woman was banging a tambourine ominously. This made me feel very self-conscious. All I was wearing was the sarong, which meant my beer belly was on display for all to see. On my small frame, my beer belly seemed out of proportion to the rest of my body, and I now felt ashamed of it.

A row of buckets were lined up in front of a drain running along most of the length of one side of the courtyard. A group of addicts were already kneeling in front of these containers. There were only three buckets without an accompanying addict and I followed *Matt* and knelt in front of one of these. The other westerners began calling out some final advice: 'Drink as much water as you possibly can,' 'Kneel on your shoes,' and 'When you feel the vomiting about to come, stick your fingers down your throat to speed it along.' I grabbed on to these bits of advice like a life-raft and I felt completely out of my depth. This was madness. What had I let myself in for? I looked around for an exit but couldn't see one through the crowd of onlookers that had surrounded us. I felt trapped and there was nowhere to flee to; I was on the verge of a panic attack.

The band was positioned in front of me and they began to fall into a rhythm, that soon turned into a song which many others in the crowd seemed familiar with:

Krao nii, dtong lerk hai dai,
Ta lerk mai dai, dtong daay ner ner,
Lerk sep-dit sia dii tii ter,
Dtit pai jon ger, kong yer sak wan.
Krai hen gaw ruu gan tua,
Taa kuin pai mua,
Dtong cha jabann,
Lerk sep-dit,
Sa-tii tua gan,
Taa lerk mai dai nan dtong daay ner ner.

I struggled to make sense of these Thai words in a bid to divert my focus from the upcoming ceremony and ease my tension:

Now is the time to quit,
If we can't quit, we are sure to die,

It is truly great to defeat our addictions,
If we keep doing it till we are old, it will get us some
day,
Doesn't matter who or where, everybody knows,
If you start doing drugs,
You need to make a vow,
To quit drugs forever,
Because if we can't quit, we are sure to die.

-

I saw that one of the brown-robed monks had already handed out medicine to the guy kneeling at the bucket furthest away from mine. It was difficult to see exactly what it was that was being handed out but the effects of the concoction were soon evident. Within seconds the kneeling man spewed, and this projectile vomit came out of him in heaves. It was powerful stuff. I had never seen anything like it.

I had taken the advice to kneel on my sneakers, but it felt uncomfortable so I removed them, but immediately I began to wriggle with the discomfort caused by the uneven cement floor. I put the sneakers back underneath my knees.

As the monk came nearer to my position I was able to see what it was he was handing out. It was a brown substance which looked just like muck, and I was terrified by it. The muck was being poured from a brown Chang Beer bottle, and it was being handed out in a shot glass. The irony wasn't lost on me. Although it seemed bizarre, I thought maybe it was also symbolic. After all, my downfall had come from these glass utensils so maybe my salvation could be found in them too. It's funny the thoughts that go through your mind at times like these. Maybe it was my brain's way of helping me cope with what was about to happen but I was glad of the momentary distraction.

The monk doling out the medicine had a solemn air and his movements were smooth and confident. He reminded me of the martial arts experts I had once envied in Chinese movies. He just seemed so purposeful and completely involved in the task at hand. He obviously took the job seriously and this increased my confidence in him and his medicine. I had a suspicious mind and it was easy for me to doubt the motives of people trying to help me. Sometimes this doubt was justified, but often it was just a means my messed-up mind used to stop me from getting the help I so desperately needed.

At last the monk arrived in front of me. I was shaking visibly by this stage. He smiled kindly at me as he handed me the brown liquid. Like Phra Hans earlier, his eyes were clear and full of understanding. I reached for the shot glass and poured it down my throat in one swallow. I knew that this was the way to take the medicine, but could not remember who had given me this instruction.

The medicine tasted even more disgusting than it looked. It only briefly touched my taste buds, but that was enough to send them into revolt. My stomach rebelled next, but this feeling passed and for a few seconds, nothing happened. I could hear the monk behind me shouting; '*gin, gin ...*' which is Thai for 'drink', so I followed these instructions. I was hit by a feeling of overwhelming sickness never before experienced in all my years of drunken vomiting. I began retching violently and could feel my stomach cramping.

The fact that the medicine did not belong inside my body became instantly clear, and for a short while the sole purpose of my existence was to remove this poison from my system. In the midst of the barrage of pain and cramping that ensued, I was left with no doubt in my mind that failure to remove even a drop of this stuff would lead to dire consequences later on. The medicine left a bitter aftertaste in my mouth.

The other westerners standing around joined in instructing me to knock back as much water as possible. I noticed two of the western observers were wearing identification badges and realised they must be temple volunteers. I looked at one of them appealingly, but it was hard to get anybody's attention when you were among a group of projectile vomiters.

I tried to follow the advice to drink as much water as I could from the silver pail in front of me. I scooped it up in a green container which was similar to what Thais use to flush their toilets. It was tricky getting the liquid inside me while I continued to retch, and vomit was now pouring out of my nose as well as my mouth. My stomach felt like it had just been kicked and I'd been winded. Putting water in there seemed counter intuitive, but I did as I'd been instructed and rammed my fingers down my throat to speed things along.

Matt was kneeling next to me, with *Sharon* on the other side of him. He was having no problem getting the water down his throat and tackled the bucket like a pro. He knocked back a full scoop of water each time, then spewed up the contents of his stomach into the drain in front of us.

Eventually the pain in my stomach began to subside and a few minutes later the vomiting eased to an occasional retch. People were standing up from their buckets and leaving the courtyard. *Matt* and *Sharon* had finished. I didn't want to be left alone, so I decided to take a chance and follow them. I fought against the urge to be sick and managed to make it across the courtyard without vomiting. On the other side I saw a hose for cleaning the buckets and a bench for storing them.

A little while later, I found *Matt* at the back of our dorm, which was also the area where the toilets and showers were located. *Matt* was already there, vomiting into an open drain. In between vomiting he was cursing the temple and his own idiocy for coming to it. I started to feel the urge to be sick again too. I went back to my room, grabbed a plastic bottle of water and joined *Matt* beside the drain. He ignored me, but we soon fell into rhythm with each other. We took turns drinking from our bottles and being sick into the drain.

The absurdity of our situation struck me, and I began to laugh. *Matt* turned and looked at me as if I were a lunatic.

'I'm glad you think it's funny. I nearly puked up one of me fucking balls!' he said.

This only made me laugh harder. We stayed there for a while, waiting for our nausea to subside, and we began swapping jokes and laughing just like school children.

CHAPTER 23

It usually took a long time for my appetite to return after quitting the booze, but I began to feel hungry only an hour after the vomiting ceremony. When I told *Matt* that I was going to see if I could find something to eat, he again looked at me as if I were insane. He agreed to join me, however, just to escape from the gloomy dorm.

We headed towards the eating area at the far end of the dormitory buildings. The rest of the patients were already sitting there and most of them were tucking into grub. The westerners were sitting together in front of the small food shack, while the Thais were spread out around stone tables further away.

Matt's other half was already there, and I took the opportunity to introduce myself properly. *Sharon* looked like a drug user. She sat huddled up in herself and puffed furiously on a cigarette. She had the potential to be really pretty, but the effects of her heroin abuse were clearly showing and she looked ravaged. *Sharon* complained bitterly about the medicine and insisted that she would not be going through the ceremony again. She found the whole thing disgusting and degrading. I empathised with her, and wondered if I would be able to repeat today's performance now that I knew what it involved. I said it was worth it if it meant escaping addiction, trying to remain as upbeat as possible.

I was contemplating what to eat, when I noticed *Matt* looking at me with disgust. 'How can you even possibly think about eating?' he asked, incredulous. *Sharon* surprised him by saying that she might try a plate of chips. I volunteered to get the food.

I went inside the dim food shack and found someone at the back. I ordered some rice soup for myself. She had offered to make whatever I wanted so long as the ingredients were available, but now was not the time to be adventurous. Rice soup was about all I could handle at the time. It wouldn't be too hard to digest and would be easy on my stomach if I needed to vomit it back up.

While waiting for the food to arrive, I got to know some of the other western patients. *Bill* was a burly Canadian who looked a bit like a Hell's Angel with his goatee. He was also a drunk, but his drug of choice had been cocaine. His charismatic air marked him out as the type of drinker who I had always aspired to be: the life and soul of the party.

Joseph was a curly-haired Greek who had come to escape his addiction from cocaine and prescription drugs. He was slightly effeminate and had a caring nature. He had been particularly encouraging and helpful during the vomiting ceremony. Despite English not being his mother tongue he spoke it flawlessly, with a BBC accent. It was hard to imagine him as an addict.

I was sad to discover that *Bill* and *Joseph* were due to leave the temple in a few days. They seemed to know their way around the temple, and I really wanted someone to take me by the hand and just tell me what I needed to do in order to beat my addiction.

George, a Glaswegian, was the oldest in our group and we had a lot in common despite our age difference. He too had gone through the ARP programme. I felt great comradeship with him straight away. Only addicts can really understand other addicts, and drunks have a special affinity with one other, which I suppose must be true for all addicts and their fellow abusers. He was a hardened drunk and, like me, this was his last attempt at giving up drink. If this failed, he too would embark on an alcohol-fuelled suicide mission.

The food arrived, and I tucked in straight away. I wanted to do all I could to speed the detox process along. I knew it would be impossible to escape the withdrawal process completely, but I wanted to make it as painless as possible.

Steve, who had accompanied *Matt* and *Sharon*, joined us at the table. He had already been through the programme and was now a success story. He was eager to help others and this explained his willingness to promote the temple.

It was obvious he had been a bit of a lad in his day. He had an easygoing attitude and always seemed to be on the verge of laughter. It was easy to imagine he had been able to hide the worst of his previous addiction through his extrovert personality. How to manipulate others is something all addicts learn to do very quickly.

Steve told me that aside from helping *Matt* and *Sharon*, he had another motivation for returning to the temple. He wanted to get some more of the herbal tea which was only available at Thamkrabok. Along with the many other medicinal benefits this tea was reputed to have, it was also said to improve liver function. *Steve* had become convinced of its usefulness in helping people like him who had contracted Hepatitis B.

Steve described how much his life had improved since he had kicked his heroin habit, and this was a helpful pep talk for those of us who were only at the beginning of our recovery. I found his positivity and hope inspirational and even *Matt*, who had been very quiet, seemed to brighten up a little. I needed to hear all the positive stories I could to keep me motivated.

As well as being a big fan of Thamkrabok, *Steve* was also a strong advocate of 12 step programme. I had long since lost faith in AA, but didn't make these feelings known. On a personal level I had a lot of respect for AA, but I had decided it would not be part of my final walk away from addiction. I didn't just want to give up alcohol, I wanted to walk away from being an alcoholic and AA would only serve as a constant reminder.

George was more vocal in his condemnation of 12 step programme, however. He snapped when *Steve* made the claim that 'involvement with the meetings was vital to permanent recovery from addiction.'

'That's rubbish, plenty of people quit alcohol and drugs without the need to go running to meetings every day. If Alcoholics Anonymous is the only way to get sober than I think that I'd prefer to be drunk in a bar. Bunch of sanctimonious fanatics.'

I didn't feel as strongly as *George*, but I could understand him. Plenty of people did get and stay sober without any help from the meetings, and the arrogance of assuming that AA was the only way to deal with recovery was just ignorance. I had once been that arrogant AA member and I didn't blame anyone for being so fanatical. I knew that thinking this way helped some people stay sober. Addiction is what led us all to AA, and AA subsequently became our new addiction. I wanted to be free from any type of addiction. I wanted a clean break.

Steve didn't respond to *George*'s attack on the 12 step programme. He changed the subject, which was a relief. *George*, however, went quiet, and his withdrawal from the conversation urged the others to bring him back into the chat.

'Has *George* told you about his first night in the temple?' *Bill* asked.

George squirmed a bit in his chair, but I could tell that he liked the attention. *Bill* told the story of how *George* had spent his first night at the temple.

Apparently *George* had arrived at Thamkrabok drunk, and in possession of a full bottle of whisky. When the monk had tried to confiscate the bottle, *George* reacted by knocking back most of the bottle.

'It would have been a shame to waste it!' *George* said.

He had spent that first night walking around the temple singing and dancing and being generally off his head. His attempts to encourage everyone else to join his party failed, and as the night wore on without further alcohol, he became aggressive and morose. He passed out just before he could get into any real trouble. *George*'s first night had made him a bit of a celebrity among the monks and the Thai patients, who still frequently made reference to his antics.

As well as turning up drunk, he also turned up a week late. Volunteers had shown up at the airport to meet him, but he had managed to evade them and went partying in Bangkok instead. Apparently this is quite common. Volunteers often go to collect people who have had second thoughts on the plane. *George* was one of the few who still somehow made it to the temple, albeit a little later than expected.

Matt was struggling to stay in the conversation and had started to shake and sweat quite noticeably. Like *Sharon*, he hugged his body and chain-smoked from the fast disappearing pack of cigarettes he shared with her. Without announcement he got up from the table and moved towards our dorm.

The others started drifting out of the eating area, and soon myself and *Sharon* were the only two left. My thoughts turned to alcohol. *Sharon* was battling with her own withdrawal, and seemed reluctant to leave the restaurant. She shared her dorm with two Thai women who spoke hardly any English. The two friendly Thais were not put off by the lack of a common language and their continued attempts at conversation were a bit much for *Sharon*.

She told me about her descent into addiction. Experimenting with a bit of hash and alcohol at 13, before being tempted by the bigger high offered by the stronger drugs. She was eager for me to know that she only smoked gear, she never injected and was determined that she never would. *Sharon* believed *Matt*'s addiction to heroin was far more serious than her own because he had a longer habit and because he injected.

Sharon confided in me that it was really for *Matt* that she had come to the temple. She still got enjoyment from her drug use, but realised she would need to walk away from it at some stage. She could see how it was destroying her life.

Sharon and I remained chatting in the restaurant for another while, and after she excused herself to return to her dorm, I was alone. I dreaded the long night which I knew was ahead of me. All too well, I knew the feeling of being ill and terrified during previous occasions of withdrawal. This fear could unexpectedly come upon me and freeze me on the spot, and was often accompanied by hallucinations or vivid dreams. I could be just walking along and then suddenly I'd see rats or cockroaches everywhere.

I didn't want to be alone so I headed back to the dorm to see what *Matt* was up to. I found him awake but silent. He was lying on his bed wearing only his boxer shorts. He was sweating heavily, and staring at the empty bed on the opposite side of the room as if there was someone there. It gave me the creeps and I thought that maybe he was seeing things. I hoped that he wouldn't freak out. Withdrawals could really mess with someone's mind and there was always the risk of them becoming violent. There was only the two of us in the room, and I had enough shit on my own plate to deal with.

That night was painfully slow. I would start to drift off to sleep, but the intense images in my dreams would startle me awake again. *Matt*'s moaning and rolling in his bed all night didn't help matters.

Lying there, it was hard not to question my decision to come to the temple. Thamkrabok did not live up to the image I had had of it in my head. I had expected it all to be easy. It seemed reasonable that once the decision to quit was made, then the journey would be all downhill. I tried to think of all the good things that would happen in my life if I managed to get sober, but in the midst of this pain, I wondered if any of it was really worth it.

CHAPTER 24

I WAS JUST drifting off to sleep when *Bill* arrived in our dormitory to announce that we needed to get up and help with the morning chores. It was still dark outside. Getting up after so little sleep was a struggle—*Matt* refused point blank. *Bill* warned *Matt* that this early morning activity was part of the treatment, to which *Matt* responded by saying: 'Go fuck yourself, I didn't travel to the other side of the world to be treated like a slave.' *Matt* had a way with words.

I followed *Bill* and we met up with *George* and *Joseph*. We made our way back to the area where the medicine had been dispensed the previous day. Some of the Thai patients started to arrive then, and we were also joined by the monks, who brought out a rack full of brushes. I followed everyone else's lead and grabbed one of these, picked a spot, and began sweeping the leaves back and forth.

I soon fell into the rhythm of sweeping. The simple action felt therapeutic, and I was thankful that I'd made the effort. We slowly worked our way around the yard as a group. The work felt satisfying, and I enjoyed seeing mountainous piles of leaves build up.

We moved from one courtyard to another and passed by our own dormitory. Looking back and seeing more leaves falling where we had just swept made our efforts seem pointless, but I tried not to think of it that way. I knew that the leaves needed to be kept under control, as they were the perfect hiding place for snakes, scorpions and disease-carrying mosquitoes. This twice daily routine was restorative and it gave me the feeling of being useful.

We continued until we reached a shrine dedicated to the founders of the temple. This was the last area that we were expected to sweep. Once finished, the patients put their brushes aside and went to pay their respects to the shrine. I followed their example and grabbed three incense sticks which I lit from a flame already burning for this purpose. I then joined the others in kneeling in front of the Buddha and bowing three times. The first bow was to the Buddha, the second to his teaching, and the third to the community of Buddhists who keep his teachings alive.

I rejoined *Joseph*, *George* and *Bill* who told me there was nothing to do for a while and that I should just relax until breakfast. This made me feel at a bit of a loss. I was now full of energy despite my lack of sleep the night before, and had no wish to go back to the room where I had spent the night tossing and turning.

I could hear the sound of *Matt* complaining as soon as I stepped through the dorm door. He had cornered

George, but when he saw me he turned his tirade in my direction.

'Have you seen the bleeding state of the toilets? How am I supposed to take a fucking shit?'

The Thai squat toilet was something that had become a familiar part of my life, but this was *Matt*'s first encounter with them. I was used to them now and they weren't that bad. Apparently they're better for you as you don't strain so much when you're squatted down. I explained this to *Matt*, who didn't look convinced. I added that he should remember to keep toilet paper handy when visiting the Thai toilet as many Thais don't use it.

'What do they use then?' *Matt* asked. I told him how they use a scoop of water and their hands.

'Dirty bastards!' was his response.

Matt returned to his bed and lay there for a while scratching his balls through his boxer shorts. I surprised myself by having enough concentration to finish a couple of chapters of my book. After a while we fell into conversation. *Matt* seemed to be in a more reflective mood and began to relate all his real fears about coming to the temple.

For many years, *Matt* had been a functioning drug user. He could hold down a job and was able to hide his problems from his work colleagues. He worked for a transport company and had managed to get a good job in which he didn't need to deal with the public. His drug habit was hardcore, but he had managed to stop using for a while before. Life without drugs had been too hard for him, however, and he worried about relapsing again this time. He wanted Thamkrabok to work for him, and he confessed that a lot of his current negativity was linked to fear. Like me, the separation of work-life and addiction was getting harder to maintain, and prior to arriving at the temple, *Matt* had been off sick from work so that he could focus completely on his habit. His physical condition was deteriorating and his finances were a mess. The enjoyment was now gone from taking the drug, but as the misery increased so did his addiction.

Matt's sudden openness had come from nowhere, but it allowed me to see that he wasn't just a complainer, and had much of the same concerns as I did. We had a lot in common, and I started to feel closer to him. He spoiled the moment though by turning the conversation back to complaints about the state of the room, the state of the temple, and the state of Thailand.

We were called to assemble for the Thai national anthem. *Matt* refused to leave his bed once again. I reminded him that we were guests in the country and the least we could do was show a little respect. He said that he 'couldn't give a fuck'. This attitude annoyed me because I knew from experience how seriously the people of Thailand took their national anthem. We were in Thailand being treated for free—it wasn't much to ask.

The anthem had only just begun when I noticed *Matt* being accompanied out of the dorm by two of the monks; he wouldn't be escaping the national anthem after all.

After this, we were on the move again. We had to collect vouchers which we would later use to buy food in the temple. As we had no money, these vouchers were given on credit and we would be expected to settle up upon leaving Thamkrabok.

The vouchers were handed out at the entrance area of the Hay. A wooden table had been set up for the purpose, and vouchers of different denominations were spread out on it. Two monks were seated on the opposite side of the table, one to keep accounts in a well-worn red ledger and the other to hand out the pretend-money.

The whole temple population was in attendance, so the handing out of vouchers took some time. They called our names one by one, and after collecting our money we queued up for the herbal tea *Steve* had been raving about. I really hoped the claims he had made about it were true, and that it could help me to repair my liver, but I wasn't sure how much I believed this. I needed a cure, but a large part of me didn't feel I deserved one.

The drink was stored in a large yellow container with a spout for us to extract the liquid. *Matt* grimaced as he drank his, saying that it, 'tasted like drinking a bleeding tree.' *Matt* wasn't exaggerating this time—it had a fairly repulsive taste but it was nowhere near as bad as the vomiting medicine. I needed the stuff to work its magic on me, so in that spirit, I finished the cup.

We were then left to our own devices for a few hours. I joined the others for breakfast and ordered rice soup again. This detox was turning out to be far different than anything I had experienced previously. In some ways the symptoms seemed far more intense than usual. Generally, they would be more spread out, and the return of my appetite so quickly was new. I saw it as a good sign. I ate my breakfast in the anticipation that this might be my last meal of the day. I wouldn't be eating after noon in preparation for the medicine show in the evening, and the thought of eating twice before midday seemed asking for a bit much.

CHAPTER 25

MATT AND I sat chatting in our dorm for a while. He remarked that he was feeling better physically, and that the medicine was leading to smoother withdrawal symptoms.

We talked about growing up in Dublin. It turned out we knew many of the same people and shared many similar experiences. I had the impression that *Matt* came from a poor background, but learned that he grew up in a fairly posh area and had a lot going for him prior to becoming hooked on drugs. He had been given the opportunities to become successful in life, but had decided to take a different path.

A little while later, a couple of monks entered our dorm. They went to the empty bed across from *Matt*, put the mattress onto the floor, and then left. It seemed like strange behaviour, and we both speculated about what they might be up to. *Matt* hoped this moving of furniture meant that someone was 'actually going to clean the fucking kip.'

I suggested that *Matt* should get something to eat, while I went to get some more herbal tea. I had decided to drink it until it came out of my ears if it could help me. I'd already managed three cups that day, and the taste was growing on me.

By the time the food arrived, *Matt* was shaking again and complaining of cramps. He had arranged to have a massage so he returned to the dorm to see if the masseuse was ready for him. I followed *Matt* back to the dorm.

The masseuse visited the temple almost every day. Massage was meant to be great for withdrawal pains. I had aches and pains all over my body, especially around my abdominal area, and hoped to get a massage too, but the masseuse only visited the temple for a couple of hours a day and so wouldn't be able to get to us all. When it had been mentioned earlier in the morning *Matt* and *Sharon* jumped at the chance of anything which would help them feel better. I knew their need was greater than mine, but still, I couldn't help but feel a little hard done by.

During *Matt*'s massage, we heard a commotion outside our door, and I spotted a jeep right outside our room. A group of monks were dragging an unconscious man out of the back of it. They were carrying him in our direction and now we understood the purpose of the mattress on the floor.

The monks manoeuvred our new friend into the room. My bed was beside the door and I managed to get a good look at him. He was in a right mess. His trousers were soaked and he had obviously wet himself. There was also the unmistakable stench of faeces and brown smudges were soaking through his pants. He was covered in yellow vomit down his front, and his hair was also speckled with vomit.

The monks positioned our new friend on his side. The rest of us were leaving for a temple activity so our cataleptic roommate would be left alone for a while. I decided to take a closer look at him before we left and was relieved to hear him snoring soundly.

WE ALL ARRIVED for our afternoon steam bath. With the heat beating down on us the idea of a steam bath seemed a little unwise. I was already soaked from head to toe in sweat before we even started, but the bath was part of the detoxification process, the aim of it being to speed things along. Special plants, unique to the temple, were added to the steam. We were joined by the Thai patients while we waited at the entrance to the Hay. When we were outside the Hay, we were divided into two groups. The Thai males formed one group, and they headed to a steam bath at another part of the temple. The foreigners were joined by the two female Thai patients and we used the steam bath straight across from the Hay.

Our steam bath was run by one of the foreign monks who turned out to be quite a character. Monk Gordon was an ex-American soldier of fortune. Apparently he had been involved in many wars and had somehow ended up in Asian conflicts. During a break from one of these wars he went touring through Thailand, and his tour bus got four flat tyres outside Thamkrabok. While he was waiting for the bus to be fixed he wandered inside the temple for something to do. The abbot spotted him, and told Gordon he had been expecting him. He said Gordon was now to stay at the temple. For some reason Gordon agreed to this and has never left. Now, many years later, he has transformed from a mercenary to a gentle Buddhist monk.

Monk Gordon accepted the plants which we had arrived with and disappeared behind the steam bath. The sauna was fairly low-tech and we had a brief wait while the monk started a fire, adding the plants so that they would mix with the steam entering the concrete chambers.

We were joined inside by Gop and the sauna quickly filled up with steam. We were wearing our sarongs and large beads of sweat were appearing on my bare chest. The heat felt like a physical presence in the room, pushing me against the wall and pinning me down on the wooden seat. Monk Gop was grinning at me, probably expecting me to flee from the heat. We were supposed to stay there until a monk outside called to say that ten minutes had passed—time seemed to have stopped.

The first one to break was *Matt*. With a now familiar 'fuck this' he left the room. I wanted to follow him, but decided to hang on for as long as possible. I just focused on my breathing. *Bill* and *Joseph* must have become acclimatised to the heat and didn't seem to be finding it too hard. They were laughing and pointing over at me. I began to worry that the monk outside had forgotten all about us. Surely ten minutes had passed long ago. At last I heard someone shout, '*awk pai*', which meant our time was up. I burst out of the room and scooped some lovely cool water over myself.

We were given a few minutes break during which time we drank some more of the herbal tea, the idea being that the sauna would help push it out of our pores to speed along the detoxification process. We soaked ourselves in cool water before once again hitting the sauna.

We had three sessions inside the sauna room and each one seemed to last an eternity, but it definitely seemed to be beneficial. On the walk back to the Hay I felt fresh and cleaner than I could ever remember feeling. My mind also seemed to have been given a clean-out and for a short while I experienced complete absence of any withdrawal symptoms.

We arrived back in the dorm to find our roommate still unconscious on the mattress. He must have recently wet himself because there were new wet patches on his trousers and the smell in the room was unbearable. *Matt*, who was not inhibited by any need to be diplomatic, shouted: 'Wake up you filthy scumbag, you're stinking the fucking place out.' I laughed nervously, but the sleeping man didn't respond.

News must have travelled about the smell in our room, however, because three monks soon arrived on the scene, accompanied by two of the female western volunteers. They set about removing the man's soiled clothing but as soon as they touched him he awoke from his slumber. He still hadn't opened his eyes but he began kicking out at everything around him. He kicked and winded one of the monks, and the volunteers intervened and tried to explain to the madman where he was and what they were doing. This did nothing to calm him down and actually excited him further. He began screaming 'Get the fuck away from me!' in a thick Welsh accent.

Matt was sitting up on his bed the whole time, enjoying the show. He thought the whole thing was hilarious and shouted out comments and advice to both the madman and those who were trying to restrain him:

'You kick like a girl!'

'Catch his legs!'

'Sit on the crazy nutter!'

'Nice one, you nearly hit his balls.'

The monks ignored *Matt*'s commentary, but one of the volunteers threw him a filthy look. I was too gobsmacked by the whole thing to intervene. After all, it's not every day you see a group of Thai monks fighting with a half-crazed Welshman. Despite the efforts to calm the man down he continued to scream and thrash about, and if anything, he appeared to become progressively more enraged.

He eventually opened his eyes and somehow managed to spring to his feet.

'Where's my stuff? Who stole my fucking stuff?' he screamed.

The monks gathered in a circle around the Welshman and, swiftly, they rushed at him and bundled him out the door. He was kicking and screaming as he went.

They led him out towards the pool and pushed him straight in. The initial shock of the cool water stunned him, but not for very long. He swam to the side of the pool and began taking swipes at the monks' legs, trying to pull them into the pool with him. The monks were too fast for him though. He soon realised the futility of his exploits, however, and he began bargaining with the monks.

'Just give me back my stuff, and I'll leave.'

One of the volunteers tried to explain to him that his stuff was locked away for the present and that he needed to stay in the temple until he at least sobered up a bit more.

'Give me back my fucking drugs or I'll destroy the place.'

The volunteers patiently explained they would not be able to give him back any drugs and that, in fact, he hadn't actually arrived with any. The man once again began thrashing around in the pool, screaming blue murder. Eventually he wore himself out and calmed down a bit.

'OK, I'll behave, just let me out of this fucking pool.'

They helped him out of the pool, and for a few seconds it seemed like calm had been restored in the temple.

The Welshman hadn't even gotten through the door of the dorm, however, when he kicked off again. He had been walking ahead of two of the monks when he started kicking the door.

'I want out of this nuthouse, give me back my stuff or you will be sorry.'

'If it's your drugs you're after you can forget it, we had them while you were sleeping,' *Matt* taunted.

Matt was joking, but the monks understood what he said and looked at him suspiciously. Our new roommate took the wind-up badly.

'You bastards, you stole my stuff. I'll fucking kill you.'

I tried to calm things down by pointing out *Matt* was joking, but the man wasn't listening. *Matt*, meanwhile, was loving the fury he was creating.

'Your gear was shit anyway.'

The man kicked the door again causing the mosquito netting to fall off. The monks had seen enough. Once again they bundled him out the door, but this time they brought him to a room on the other side of the courtyard. They locked the Welshman inside. He continued screaming and shouting and banging for 30 minutes. Eventually he wore himself out again.

After a further 30 minutes the volunteers opened the room and went inside. A little while later they came out accompanied by a much calmer Welshman.

He was aware of his audience, however, and raised his fist in the air shouting: 'Free at last! Free at last!' We assumed after all the fuss that the man had decided to check himself out, and so we were surprised when he arrived back in the Hay, having just taken his *satja* vow.

CHAPTER 26

WHEN I RETURNED to the dorm after the afternoon sweep of the temple, the Welshman was inside arguing with *Matt*, but it all seemed to be in good humour. His name was *Danny*, and he was from Cardiff. Even though he had taken the *satja* vow he still didn't want to stay in the temple. I asked him why he had bothered taking the vow, and he claimed he had been tricked into it. *Matt* responded with exactly what I was thinking: 'Bullshit!'

In between demanding to be given his drugs and to be released from the temple, *Danny* told us his story. The volunteers had gone to the airport to pick him up as he had arranged with them to do. On the plane over he had been drinking heavily and had smuggled drugs onto the plane. *Danny* made sure to bring plenty to last the trip and ended up in a real happy place.

When he'd arrived in the airport, and somehow made it through immigration, he noticed the volunteers holding up a placard with his name on it. But *Danny* had decided to continue his partying in Bangkok. He tried to evade those waiting for him but the volunteers were experienced and spotted him easily. He admitted that he was indeed the person they were looking for, but that he wanted to delay his detoxification. The volunteers managed to talk him into the van, saying that he could have a couple of bottles of vodka for the ride. Apparently, for the first part of the journey he had enjoyed sitting in the back of the van admiring the Thai scenery. His excesses soon caught up with him, however, and he passed out.

Matt quizzed *Danny* about the drugs he had claimed to be missing and the Welshman became a bit bashful. He admitted that he had forgotten, in his moments of madness, that he had actually taken everything on the plane. The fact that *Danny* had so easily taken hard drugs onto an aeroplane surprised me. It sounded to me like an outrageously dangerous thing for people to do. I couldn't understand how he could take such a risk so lightly.

Regardless of the state he was in when he arrived at the temple, *Danny* did not believe himself to have any real problem with addiction. He said that he just wanted to get off heroin, and his motivation for doing so was to get his ex-girlfriend back. I remembered feeling the same way myself at 20 years old when I had first sought help in a treatment centre, but I had since learnt that I couldn't stay sober for anybody else but me. I considered sharing this with *Danny*, but then realised there would be no point. That was a lesson he would have to learn by himself.

Danny frequently interrupted his tale by demanding that his belongings to be returned to him. He said he wanted to leave Thamkrabok, but seemed more preoccupied with talking about leaving than with actually doing anything about it. He was like a broken record. At one stage he got back out of his bed and gave the door another kick, causing the mosquito netting to collapse once more.

Matt questioned *Danny* about his drug habit and ridiculed his responses. I have no idea how much heroin is normal for a user to take on a daily basis but *Matt* scoffed at the amounts *Danny* was claiming. He accused *Danny* of being a liar, and said his boast that he had drank over two bottles of vodka before arriving at the temple was bullshit.

'You just can't handle your alcohol, same as this other gobshite beside me.'

Matt then moved on to questioning *Danny* about his sexual orientation and made derogatory remarks about the Welsh. Throughout all of these insults *Danny* tried to give back as good as he got. He spat out: 'You stupid Paddy fucker!' more than once.

Nevertheless, *Matt* had the upper hand in this battle of insults. *Danny* didn't have the mental clarity to be firing witty retorts, but they both seemed to be enjoying the exchange and *Danny* was complaining a lot less about the temple and his lack of a means to get high. Some of their wisecracks would have made a football hooligan blush, but there was nobody around to hear so I didn't see the harm. Growing up in Dublin we often insulted our friends, or their mothers or sisters. It was our way of expressing affection.

The electric bell rang again—it was time for us to take the medicine. *Danny* showed very little interest in this and his lack of curiosity about the ceremony surprised me. He just followed along with *Matt* and me, and dressed himself in the sarong. We made our way to the courtyard where the ceremony was to take place again.

The medicine show had been at the back of my mind all day. I wasn't particularly looking forward to it, as you might well imagine. The previous day I had approached the ceremony with trepidation because I didn't know what to expect. However, now I knew exactly what was involved and I was dreading it. I tried to convince myself it would be easier this time, but I didn't believe it for a minute. Despite her protestations from the day before, *Sharon* had also decided to go through the ordeal again.

Danny knelt at the bucket next to mine with *Matt* on his other side. I worried that *Danny* might react badly to the severity of the medicine and make some sort of a scene. I really hoped he wouldn't. It was bad enough having to deal with vomit coming out my nose without having to protect myself from a projectile-vomiting maniac who was freaking out beside me.

The music started and, exactly as before, the medicine-man went from one patient to the next, handing out the puke-inducer. I turned to *Danny* and tried to fire some last-minute advice his way, but

Danny seemed to be in a world of his own and wasn't listening to anybody.

Once again my hand shook as I accepted the medicine. I tried to prepare myself better than the last time, but as soon as the drink hit my taste buds I started to panic.

I started knocking back scoops of water and out of the corner of my eye, I could see *Danny* taking his medicine. For a brief moment my curiosity about how he would react took my mind off my own problems. The medicine couldn't be ignored for long though, and I rammed my fingers down my throat to speed the vomit along.

Danny was knocking the water back like it was something he had been born to do. He moved over the gutter and belched loudly as he put his fingers in his mouth. He took a few moments to loudly curse the temple and all its inhabitants before he hit the water again. I noticed that the monks had all congregated near *Danny*. They were probably just as wary of how he would react to the medicine as I was. The volunteers looked on from a safer distance, watching apprehensively.

Occasionally I caught a glimpse of *Matt* and *Sharon*, poor *Sharon* seemed to be having a dreadful time of it. She had tears in her eyes and was trying hard to get the water down her neck. It was difficult to distinguish between her sobs and her retches.

Matt seemed to be doing the best out of all of us. He was swallowing bucketloads of water. Under normal circumstances he might have got a kick out of *Danny*'s discomfort but, like me, he had his own concerns to deal with.

I was struggling. It was worse than the previous day. My stomach was cramping, and I just couldn't drink enough water to speed the process along quickly enough. My stomach felt like it was about to burst, and I gagged when any water touched the back of my neck. For a while, all that was coming up when my fingers hit my throat was air. I began to think that the medicine might be lethal.

Eventually, the water managed to mix with the medicine in my stomach and my vomit became more substantial. My cramps began to ease until they finally stopped completely. I convinced one of the monks that I was well enough to leave the courtyard and he allowed me to take my bucket and put it away. This time I was one of the first to leave.

I could see the benefit of vomiting in front of a group of strangers. Maybe that is the real secret of the temple's success. It is hard to have an inflated opinion of yourself when you are in such a vulnerable position. Once the self-importance is removed we all become more open to offers of help. I think the killer combination with addicts is low self-worth coupled with complete self-absorption.

Despite these supposed benefits of the public vomiting sessions, I still preferred to do the last of my puking back at the dorm. This time *Danny* joined *Matt* and me around the gutter. We could hear *Sharon* vomiting up the last of her medicine. She was alone as the Thai girls had already finished. I felt sorry for her having to miss out on the social aspect of the vomiting session. I know it sounds bizarre but at the time it felt so natural standing around knocking back our drinks and taking turns vomiting into the gutter—sort of like a good night at the pub! In the midst of his heaves *Danny* continued to make threats about what would happen if he wasn't allowed to leave the temple and if they didn't give him his stuff back.

THE IDEA THAT we were kept in the temple against our will is just a myth. We could leave any time we wanted. The front of the Hay has a big gate with sturdy iron fencing, but the back is open and it would have been easy to leave that way. The thing really keeping us there was the fact that we had nowhere else to go.

My appetite returned as the medicine completely left my body. *Danny* joined us in the restaurant, and to *Matt*'s astonishment, he ordered some Thai food. This further convinced *Matt* that *Danny*'s withdrawals were nowhere near as bad as he was making them out to be.

Danny continued to make threats and demands for the rest of the evening. He would tell his tale of woe to anyone who would listen, and as soon as a new face appeared on the scene he would repeat his performance. He particularly sought out the monks, believing he could achieve better results with them.

The monks played it cool with him. They did things Thai style. Rather than saying 'no' to him they would listen patiently and tell him they would see what they could do.

Bill and *Joseph* were in high spirits that evening as it was their last night in the temple. They were full of hope for the future and were keen to share this with the rest of us. Hearing them talk about their dreams gave me a boost. I wanted to complete the treatment like they had and leave the temple with a brighter future to look forward to.

Back in the dorm the two boys resumed their slagging match. *Danny* had been promoted from a mattress on the floor to a proper bed. He was directly across from *Matt*, but they shouted at each other as if they were separated by a great distance. They both began comparing their withdrawal pains, each downplaying the misery of the other.

It was getting near 10pm and neither *Matt* nor *Danny* showed any signs of quietening down. Bangs were coming from the room next door. Only a thin partition separated us, and frequent barrages of curses aimed in our direction accompanied the banging.

I hadn't slept much the previous night and was exhausted by then. Up until now the two boys had been a great source of entertainment but I was so tired by that stage I felt sick. My expectations for that night hadn't been high, but I had hoped for a bit of rest at least. My irritation with the lad's banter was reaching boiling point. I was used to spending long periods of time alone or at least in silence. I liked to laugh and talk with Oa, but I always managed to get away by myself for a few hours each day. Since arriving at the temple I hadn't had any time to myself and there hadn't even been the break that sleep would have provided.

There was no sign that my roommates were going to settle down any time soon, so I took my book outside and sat reading by myself for a while. On my way back to the dorm a little while later, *George* cornered me. He looked furious and demanded that I tell the other two to put out the light in the room and keep the noise down. It felt like he was blaming me for their behaviour and I told him that I would mention it, but I resented having to do his dirty work. *Bill* and *Joseph* were wide awake too but they didn't seem too bothered by the noise; they were leaving for more comfortable accommodation the next day.

I passed on the message to the lads and predictably they reacted as though I was the one complaining. I was pissed off with the noise but knew that bitching about it wouldn't help matters. I reminded them I was just the messenger.

'There is no way that I'm putting the light out, and going to sleep at half ten at night and if that miserable old git doesn't like it, he can go fuck himself.'

I could see that *George* was a guy who liked things to go a certain way, and if they didn't, then he would take it badly. Things were not going too well for him now but I felt that he had made a tactical error by complaining to the lads because, if anything, they became noisier over the next hour and the bright neon light, which served both our rooms, remained on. As the clock ticked away *George* wasn't alone in his fury. I was becoming more and more annoyed as the night wore on, but I kept my mouth shut. Eventually, however, I just couldn't take it anymore and decided to take my bedding to the next room to see if I could at least get a nap there.

Despite *George*'s complaints, his room was an oasis of tranquillity compared to what I had just left. You could see the neon light from next door, but it wasn't as harsh, and at least the partition drowned out some of the noise. I felt relief as I put my bedding down on the floor and prepared for a bit of much needed sleep. My plan was thwarted by *George*, who informed me that I couldn't stay in that room because I hadn't finished the five days of medicine yet. What the fuck? What was it to him where I stayed? I grabbed my bedding back off the floor and headed back to the other side of the partition.

'You're right. He is a miserable old git,' I grumbled, loud enough for *George* to hear.

Before arriving at the temple, the only knowledge I had about coming off heroin was from the movies, with the film *Trainspotting* being my main source of information. What I hadn't imagined though, was that it would occur with a constant running commentary. The two lads never shut up comparing their symptoms.

They kept on rating the intensity of their current cramps, in constant competition with one another.

Eventually I could no longer hold my tongue and I pleaded with the two of them to at least turn off the fucking neon light. It was now well after midnight. They each gave me a look that said, 'How could you be so cruel?' They reluctantly agreed though, and the light above our beds disappeared in a click.

The hours began to pass by, and I had given up completely on any hope that sleep would be on the cards. I lay there consumed by rage and self-pity. I was so frustrated that I considered leaving the temple and just to rub salt in my wounds, *Matt* and *Danny* both fell asleep and were snoring soundly when *Bill* arrived to call us for our morning chores. They refused to wake up and we decided to leave them in the land of nod. I wasn't in the mood for more confrontation.

As I swept the grounds the repetitiveness of the task began to work its magic on me and I found some peace at last. I could feel my mind becoming more alert and my energy levels increasing. By the end of the sweep, I was smiling and feeling a hell of a lot more positive about life at the temple.

CHAPTER 27

IT WAS NOW my third day at the temple and my withdrawal symptoms had all but disappeared. I credited the medicine with this, and saw it as the final proof of its effectiveness. I said this to *Matt*, and he cautiously ventured that although his withdrawal from heroin had been a miserable affair, it had been easier than previous attempts. *Sharon* was more effusive in her appreciation of the medicine and claimed she too was almost symptom-free.

I managed to get a massage after breakfast. I told the masseuse about my abdominal pain and she seemed to know exactly what to do. She arrived to our session with what looked like hot stones wrapped in cloth. She massaged my stomach and the movements and hot stones started to release gas. My abdomen relaxed and the pain subsided. It was amazing really. I had suffered this abdominal discomfort almost constantly for the last few years and I was in awe of the masseuse's ability.

At some stage during the morning *Bill* and *Joseph* had left. I hadn't had a chance to say a final goodbye. I envied them their nice hotel and the chance for a peaceful sleep in an air-conditioned room. They had planned to spend a few days on a beach together in Thailand before heading back to their own countries.

I was back in the now familiar position of lying on my bed reading while *Matt* scratched away in the next bed. We were disturbed by a noise coming from the yard outside our room and we saw that the monks were setting up for a medicine show outside. What was going on? This was so typically Thai. I had grown accustomed to plans changing in Thailand and not being informed until the very last minute. When I first arrived in the county the spontaneity of the culture really appealed to me. I have since come to believe, however, that the things we find alluring about a place when we visit on holiday become the things that really bug us when we live there full-time.

Matt was about to go ballistic when *George* arrived on the scene bearing the welcome news that we would not be expected to join in this particular session. This was just a demonstration of the medicine show. It was being put on for the benefit of some visiting school children in order to teach them about the dangers of drug use. This type of exhibition occurred at least once a week at the temple according to *George*, and people travelled from all over Thailand to see the Thamkrabok patients vomit.

Although we were not expected to take the medicine we were expected to join everyone else in supporting those who were. We would be on display so the Thai students would be suitably impressed to see foreigners travelling from all over the world to get help at Thamkrabok.

The students were all in their early teens. The temple had chosen their best vomiters for the demonstration. These were Thai patients who had been at the temple for months because they had nowhere else to go, or because they would be arrested if they left. They had honed the art of getting sick to an impressive level. I stood with the other westerners feeling awkward. I looked at the fresh-faced students and felt ashamed of myself.

After the show, we were introduced to the Thai students. I was mortified when the monks told them I was a teacher in Thailand. They squealed with delight and began interrogating me in both English and Thai, asking how a teacher could end up in such a place. I was sitting on one of the concrete benches with a congregation of students around me. It all felt too much and I wanted to run away, but once again I was trapped by the crowd. The students were all from rich families, and they seemed to think that the fact that I was in a rehabilitation centre gave them the right to speak to me with disrespect. I heard one of them refer to me as '*farang kii nok*' —sticky-bird-shit foreigner— a term reserved for lowlife westerners. As soon as a gap appeared in the crowd around me I made my escape and went back to the dorm.

WE HAD TWO new arrivals that afternoon. I came back from sweeping to find a new guy in the bed on the other side of *Matt*. I welcomed him to the dorm, and he grunted in response. I asked him a few questions, but he just looked at me blankly. He was a middle-aged man, with a shiny bald head and a mean look on his face that I thought made him look like a football hooligan.

Matt and *Danny* soon returned and they were more forceful in their questioning of the new arrival. It turned out that his failure to respond to any of our questions was because he had limited English. He was German, and he seemed a bit overwhelmed by his admission. His name was *Oscar*, and he too had come with his wife. *Danny* had spotted her earlier and reckoned she was a bit of a babe. When I saw her I had to admit that she was quite attractive.

The vomiting ceremony didn't feel any easier physically for me this time than it had any of the other times, but the fact that we were now halfway through the medicine treatment made it easier to cope mentally.

As first-timers, *Oscar* and his wife reacted predictably. The woman left the area in tears with the volunteers consoling her. Phra Hans had been able to give them all the information in their own language so they weren't as lost as they looked. Still, as we had all learned, the actual experience of the medicine was altogether more intense than merely hearing about it.

When we got back to the gutter behind the dorm *Oscar* seemed far more open to any advice we might have. He looked like he might have done just about anything to get the medicine out of his body. Our little group of men around the communal vomiting pit was growing by the day.

At the restaurant that evening we got to know the two new arrivals a bit better. *Oscar*'s wife was called *Raphael* and she had a much better grasp of the English language than her husband. She was very frank and open about what brought them to the temple. As we got to know each other a bit better, *Oscar* became more comfortable speaking English, and he was quick to correct *Raphael* when he thought she was misrepresenting their story.

Oscar worked for a big German media outlet, and it was through his work he had met *Raphael*. They became a couple, and it wasn't long before *Oscar* found out that *Raphael* had a secret alcohol problem. A few months into their marriage she stopped leaving their apartment and started to spend her days drinking bottles of vodka. Rather than getting *Raphael* help, *Oscar* had taken a career break and just joined her. He wasn't much of a drinker prior to meeting his wife, but he was soon as dependent on alcohol as she was. They stayed like that for two years with *Oscar* only leaving their apartment to buy more booze and bits of food. He grew dissatisfied with this empty existence,

however, and he missed his old life. *Oscar* gave his wife
a choice: either they get help together, or they split up
and he'd get help alone. Like me, he had come across
the temple while surfing the Internet.

Oscar and *Raphael* sat with us for almost an hour
before moving to a table by themselves. *Danny* had
been paying *Raphael* a lot of attention which started
to bother *Oscar*. He turned to his wife and they had a
brief exchange in German before excusing themselves
and moving to another table.

I BEGAN TO feel happy just to be in the temple. There
was nowhere else I needed to be. All my life, up until
that point, I had always wanted to be somewhere else
or to get something else. My mind was always restless,
and I was never happy to be where I was. I was always
thinking about which bar to go to next. I'd be sitting in
a bar, planning to go to another bar. Drinking at home,
I'd want to be in a bar. Drinking in a bar, I'd want to be
drinking at home. That was the aim of meditation—to
be in the now. Here in the temple, I could achieve this
state effortlessly, and this focus on the present was the
cause of so much pleasure for me.

CHAPTER 28

IT WAS NOW day five—near the halfway mark of my stay at the temple. This scared me a little. I was happy with my progress, but felt nowhere near ready to tackle the real world and normal life by myself. Many people spend a month in the Hay. *George* had already stayed at the temple three weeks and seemed in no rush to leave. *Matt*, *Danny*, and *Sharon* all planned to stay for at least another few weeks.

The temple offered comradeship and protection from temptation. Both of these would be missing in my normal life. My plan to only stay at the temple for ten days now seemed a bit insufficient. The problem was that I didn't have any extra time to play with. I was due to return to Ireland for a working holiday in a couple of weeks and I needed to return to the village. I had some things to sort out and I wanted to spend some time with Oa before I had to leave again. My stay at the temple was passing far too quickly, and I wished I was able to freeze time so I could just relax there until I felt ready to face reality. Worrying about leaving Thamkrabok became my main focus over the next few days—the only real irritation in my otherwise peaceful existence.

MATT WAS NOW joining in with the temple chores. This had more to do with *Danny*'s involvement in them than my motivational chats. Still, it was good to see him making the effort. *Danny* and *Matt* approached the task of sweeping like it was a purely social event.

My fifth and final dose of the medicine arrived. It was the most challenging physically because, again, I just couldn't seem to drink enough water. Afterwards, I was ecstatic that I had completed the full course. This joy was tinged with sadness, however. The medicine ceremony had been the most stressful aspect of my time at the temple, but it had also provided me with so much benefit. In a strange way I always felt like a bit of a champion while taking the medicine in front of the large crowd offering their encouragement. I would miss that. Now, I was attending the ceremony as part of the audience, supporting *Danny*, *Oscar*, and *Raphael*.

One afternoon, *Danny* came back to the room fuming, and once again, he took it out on our door, which he kicked on his way in. I was so startled by this abrupt arrival that I leapt off my bed. The cause of *Danny*'s anger was that the monks had refused him permission to ring his girlfriend, or even to send her an email. He had come to the temple to win her back and wanted some idea as to how she was taking the news that he was in recovery. She had actually given him the money to come to Thailand on the condition that he never contact her again. He was confident, however, that this was only a temporary rejection and once she saw the new clean *Danny*, she would welcome him back with open arms.

The love of *Danny*'s life was more than just his partner—she had supported him financially for the last few years. She came from money, but most of this had flown in *Danny*'s direction in recent years. He admitted that being looked after financially was great, but that wasn't his reason for being with her.

The temple's rule was that there was to be no contact with the outside world during the five-day period while we were taking the medicine. After this, there were only two days of the week when a phone would be available to us. Having no news coming in or going out could make you feel a bit cut off.

I could sympathise with *Danny* because I was eager to get in touch with my own girlfriend. I was anxious to assure Oa that I had made it to the temple and that I was safe. I was told that if she rang the temple, the staff would not even be able to confirm that I was there. As far as Oa was concerned, I could be off getting drunk somewhere—or lying dead somewhere. I pleaded for a volunteer to send a message to Oa on my behalf, just to tell her that I was doing fine. I was relieved when the volunteer agreed.

SHARON WAS REALLY starting to come out of herself and it was remarkable how much coming off drugs was changing her appearance. She was a beautiful, fresh-faced, bubbly woman, completely different from the defeated-looking girl I had first met. She had become optimistic about the future and discussed her plans with us. She had her whole life in front of her, and I had to stop myself from being envious about all the opportunities youth held in store for her. Out of us all, *Sharon* really got the temple's message and she became a new person. Just being around her boosted my own positivity.

George was also a great source of inspiration to us all. He had been in the temple the longest of all the westerners. He was a good listener, and he didn't lecture, which was a relief. He had great understanding and would give concrete advice. It was obvious that *George* had been around the block a few times and he knew what he was talking about.

George's life had been rough and he had spent a lot of time on the streets. He found a peaceful way of life in the temple and, like me, he was loathe to give it up. He talked about becoming a monk and spending more time at Thamkrabok, and we all agreed this was a great idea. The problem was that he had a girlfriend who was coming to meet him in a couple of weeks in Bangkok, so he would need to delay his exit from the world, although he said he definitely planned to ordain one day.

Oscar and *Raphael* were always friendly, but spent most of their time together chatting away in their common language. They had become accustomed with spending almost every second together before arriving at the temple, so it probably was the only way that they could manage their stay. It was easy to see that *Oscar* idolised *Raphael* and that he would struggle without her. She seemed equally dependent on him. If one failed they might bring the other down with them. *Matt* and *Sharon* could face the same problem, although they didn't live in each other's pockets half as much as the other two.

The dorm became a bit more peaceful as we all got over the worst of our withdrawals. *Oscar* went through whatever withdrawal symptoms he had wordlessly. I was also able to get some sleep at night, and my nights were only restless now because of my own worries and concerns. Reaching the end of our five days meant that we could now move into the big room which *George* had had all to himself up until now.

Danny, however, pleaded with us to stay with him in the smaller dorm, so we didn't move. Word got back to the monks that we were still in the small room and they enquired as to why we hadn't moved. We asked the monks if we could stay together, and as there were no newcomers due to arrive, they agreed to leave us there for the time being. As soon as any new arrivals came we would need to move to the bigger room.

Danny and *Sharon* arranged for Phra Hans to come and teach us meditation. This was usually taught to the patients automatically, but the Swiss monk had been unusually busy recently and didn't have as much time to devote to these instruction sessions. As we were requesting it, he would make time to see us.

I approached our beginner's meditation class a little arrogantly. None of the others had ever attempted meditation, but I felt that my previous experience meant that I was far from a beginner. We had the session in a room which held a shrine to the Buddha. We were directed to find a comfortable position. I made a big show of sitting in a lotus position, hoping this would demonstrate to Phra Hans that I was already an expert. It took the rest of them a while to find a comfortable position with *Matt* and *Danny* cursing as they struggled to find a way to sit that they could maintain for a while.

Phra Hans gave an introduction to Buddhism and meditation. He was quick to explain that there would be no need to become Buddhist in order to get the benefit from meditation. He made the message seem so simple and the path of meditation seem almost easy. I later heard that he had spent years in almost solitary meditation. My arrogance reduced as I realised there was a lot I could learn from this monk.

ON THE SIXTH night there was an England versus Portugal football match on television. We were all invited to watch it around the front desk. Even *Sharon* was allowed out from her dorm later than usual. The woman's room was usually locked at 9pm. She was really excited with the prospect of staying up late.

Most of the western monks were English, so they were supporting the English team. To even things up the rest of us gave vocal support to Portugal and exchanged some good-natured banter with the English supporters.

I enjoyed the first half of the match, but then crept away to my favourite hide-out in the temple, the area behind the dorm where the showers were located. I got myself comfy with some snacks and soft-drinks and slipped away into a world of fiction. It felt great to just sit there alone, enjoying my book and my own company, without constant fears and worries running through my mind.

CHAPTER 29

OUR CONTACT WITH the Thai patients was limited due to the fact that we were on different schedules and lived in different parts of the Hay. The only time we really spent together was during the group activities. I would sometimes try to converse with them in Thai, but we seldom got past the most basic niceties. This was mainly due to my difficulties with the Thai language. I was actually surprised by how difficult I was finding it to learn Thai. So, by and large, we didn't have that much contact with the Thai patients. Flower and Nit were the exceptions, the two women who shared a room with *Sharon*. Nit was Flower's aunt and they had both come to the temple to escape their addictions; Nit was addicted to pot and opium while Flower was addicted to *yaba*.

Yaba means 'crazy medicine' in English and it is a methamphetamine. Thai people once referred to it as *yama*, which means 'horse medicine', because it allowed you to work all night. They soon realised, however, that this extra energy came with a price—it drove you crazy. *Yaba* was seen as one of the most dangerous threats to Thai society and the news was full of stories of people killing themselves or others while taking the drug. *Yaba* made you both paranoid and delusional. I had been told by monk Gop that it wasn't just the *yaba* that caused the problem, but the fact that most people sniffed paint thinner to come down from the drug. This solvent is what really fried people's brains. Almost all of the Thai patients had come to the temple because of abuse of this drug. Some of them looked as though they were beyond help. They would spend all of their time staring vacantly into space. Some of the Thai patients had stayed in the temple for years like this. They had nowhere else to go.

Luckily Flower seemed to have escaped the worst of the longterm effects of *yaba* abuse. She was intelligent and interested in the world. Her English was limited, but she was very patient with my Thai and we were able to have quite meaningful conversations. She lived in Lampang with her two-year-old daughter. She didn't blame anybody but herself for her fall into addiction. Her mother had left her father to go with a rich German, and it was at this time that Flower had begun hanging around with a bad crowd. Her new friends introduced her to the drug. Flower was plump but with a very attractive face. She laughed a lot, and found almost everything funny.

Nit was in her 40s and didn't seem like the type to use drugs. She was motherly and enjoyed fussing over Flower and *Sharon*, or anybody else who was nearby.

Her drug abuse wasn't as serious as Flower's. She smoked cannabis most days but only used opium very rarely. She never said it, but I suspected that most of the reason for her coming to the temple was to support Flower. Women using drugs was shocking to most Thai people. Outside of the areas which catered for sex tourists it was extremely rare to see women even smoking cigarettes.

CHAPTER 30

My LAST DAY at the temple arrived, and I was in a foul mood. Negative feelings had been building up in me over the previous few days, and not knowing what was going to happen once I left the temple scared me shitless. How would I handle it? Could I handle it? I dealt with these worries by withdrawing from my fellow patients in the temple. I didn't want to admit that I felt anything other than complete confidence. I have never been very good at hiding my emotions, my face always betrays me, so I tried to keep out of people's way, but this was almost impossible in the confined space of the Hay.

That evening I snapped at *Matt* after he aimed one of his insults my way: 'Thank God we won't have to look at your miserable face for much longer.'

'Why don't you go fuck yourself?' I said, storming off to my sanctuary near the showers. I was fuming but I knew he had been joking and my anger had nothing to do with *Matt*. I simply didn't want to leave the temple. I didn't feel ready and I was worried I might start drinking again. I had let myself down so many times in the past.

Matt soon came to check up on me. He was in a more serious mood, which was unusual for him. He asked me what was going on, and I opened up about my concerns. He listened without comment. When I was finished he gave his verdict. He said the fact that I was worried was a good thing because it meant I was taking the whole business seriously. He had been impressed by my determination to stay sober since coming to the temple. His words touched me, and I felt grateful, but I was still worried.

Later that evening I conducted my last official business with the temple. I had requested to repeat my *satja* vow. I was so out of it on my first attempt that I wanted to reaffirm it now that I was sober. Technically, I couldn't make the vow twice, but the monks allowed me to repeat it as a reminder to myself.

The mood in the restaurant that evening was sombre, but occasional bursts of laughter helped to lift it. I hated saying goodbye to my friends. We had been through a special time together and had seen the best and the worst in each other. It was a real struggle not to break down in tears. I would miss them all and I swore to keep in touch. I envied them for being able to stay a little longer at the temple.

I couldn't sleep that night, I was too nervous. In desperation I went for a wander around the Hay. I wanted an opportunity to say a final farewell to a place I had grown to love. In the middle of that still night, the temple seemed to speak to me. It seemed to be on my side. I walked to all parts of the temple saying my goodbyes. So much had happened there in such a short time. I was now part of something far bigger than myself.

While I was walking, I felt a surge of positivity hit me from out of nowhere. I replayed in my mind all the episodes of my life that had led me to the temple. I realised that it all had to happen as it did. It all fitted together perfectly. If even one part of my story was altered I would not be at the temple. I was being given a new start in life. This was something that was not available to everybody. Some people never fell into addiction, but still lived miserable lives full of fear and hate. My journey had brought me through highs and lows, but it had made me a better person. Rather than being my downfall, my addiction had in a way been my saviour. I understood what it was like to be completely defeated and to be willing to let go. I knew my life would never be the same again. I was never going to drink again. My journey was going in a new direction. I had no reason to be afraid. I wandered around the temple feeling excited and happy about the future. I remember how the abbot referred to the temple as an 'airport to Nirvana', and I could now agree with this sentiment. I went back to bed and slept soundly.

When I was ready to leave early the next morning, the monks were waiting for me with my motorbike. They wished me luck, and I rode away without looking back. I did one final circuit of the outer grounds of the temple and rode away from Thamkrabok.

CHAPTER 31

As I MOVED further and further away from the temple I had several realisations. The most important of these was that my journey had not finished at Thamkrabok, it had just changed direction. I was on a new path and I felt sure this would take me where I needed to go. Phra Hans had told me that simply being on this new path was enough, and there was no need to rush and miss out on the journey.

I pulled over to the side of the road and telephoned Oa. It was after 7am and I knew she would be awake. I felt incredibly nervous as I dialled the number. I had no idea how she would react to my call, and I hoped she had received the text message the Thamkrabok volunteer had promised to send to her. It pained me to think she might not have gotten the text and had spent the last ten days worrying about my whereabouts and physical condition.

Oa answered the phone after just one ring—she must have been waiting for my call. At first, it was a little strange hearing her voice again. I had changed so much since I'd last spoken to her, but she sounded exactly as she always did. I said nervously, 'Hello Oa, it's me.' I hoped I could convince her that everything would be different this time and that she'd believe how much I had changed. I felt uncomfortable and self-conscious but I was so glad to be able to talk to her again and was soon overcome with emotion. I felt happier than I ever had and I began to chat excitedly. I babbled on about how wonderful Thamkrabok had been, and that my problems with alcohol were now behind me. I knew I was being incoherent, but I wasn't able to hold back. I hoped she wouldn't mistake my excitement for drunkenness. She laughed and told me '*Jai yen yen sii*,' meaning 'calm down'. It was so good to hear her laugh, and I couldn't wait to get home and hold her again.

'You're sure that you're a good man now, *na*? No longer drunken Paul, *na*?'

'I've sworn off it for life. Even if the Buddha appeared before me and ordered me to drink, I would tell him to piss off!'

'Cola misses you too much. She misses kanom,' Oa continued, giggling happily. I laughed at this, and agreed that my dog was as likely to miss her doggy treats as much as she would me. I always bought her doggy snacks during my weekly trips to the city and without me at home she would have to go without.

I promised Oa I would rush straight home and when our conversation ended I mounted my motorbike with a new sense of purpose. I couldn't wait to start my new life and I finally felt free from my addiction. I guessed that the journey from the temple to my home in Chat Trakan would take me about six hours, so I figured I'd arrive not long after noon; 400km is a long way on a small motorbike but I didn't care. I kept the speedometer needle above 80mph the whole way and the distance soon shortened.

As I travelled, I thought more about the future. I knew if I followed through with my *satja* then good things would happen for me. I remembered the surge of positivity and certainty about the future I had experienced the previous night while wandering around the temple. I put my faith in this but remembered Phra Hans's warning that my future might not turn out exactly as I expected it to. He told me to keep my *satja* and to be patient and wait for my path to take care of me.

When I eventually reached Chat Trakan, Oa and my dog Cola were waiting outside the house for me. I felt like a returning hero but I suppose I had every right to be proud. I had just conquered an addiction that had come very close to destroying my life. As Cola barked and jumped excitedly around me, I told Oa about all that had happened over the last ten days and how grateful I was for everything the monks at Thamkrabok had done for me. Oa seemed genuinely delighted that the temple had been a success, but I knew it would take time to win her trust completely.

I told her about my friends from the temple and she laughed at my stories. She particularly enjoyed the story about *Danny*'s arrival at the temple, but was shocked that somebody would try to hit a monk.

I had been given medicine by the monks to help aid my recovery at home and that evening I took some. It tasted revolting but made me feel close to the temple again. I was glad to have it and hoped it would help to heal my liver. I wanted to live a full life and was determined to do everything in my power to get healthy.

Over the next few days my meditative practice took form. In the beginning, 15 minute meditation sessions seemed like an eternity and my mind was all over the place. I spent most of the time daydreaming. I wasn't too disappointed with this though. I knew from my previous attempts that this was just part of the course and it would likely get worse before it got better. I finished my first session and was pleased with myself for making a start at what I believed would be an important part of my future. A healthy mind would be a mind far less likely to fall back into addiction.

ONE DAY A few months later I realised that I had stopped thinking about alcohol. This was a hugely significant realisation for me as my whole life before the monastery had revolved around alcohol. When I was drinking, I was always thinking about where to go for my next drink or how to hide my drunkenness, and I spent the rest of my time thinking about how I could quit alcohol.

Alcohol had been the focus of my life since my late teens. Even during the two year period when I had stopped with the help of AA, I spent most of my time thinking about my addiction, and not drinking had become my focus instead of drinking. Now, however, I would go for weeks at a time without ever thinking about alcohol. As it had only been a short while since I'd gotten sober, I viewed this as a major accomplishment and it added to my confidence that I had finally found something that could work for me.

I had bought a CD from the temple before I'd left and it was full of songs about Thamkrabok. I recognised two of the tracks specifically because they had been sung at the vomiting ceremonies. Listening to these tracks took me right back to the monastery, and one song in particular, called *Lerk hai dai*, left me with tears in my eyes when I first listened to it. They were not so much tears of sadness, but tears of gratitude. I owed so much to the temple and I was proud to have an association with it.

The memories of the vomiting ceremony were still fresh in my mind. The ceremony had been such a pivotal part of my recovery from addiction and had helped me to get rid of the badness that had been in my head, as well as my body, for so long. It was the root of my transformation. In a strange way I missed the ceremony and I could better understand why some monks at the temple continued to perform the ritual long after their addiction had been cured. It was good for your health, both mentally and physically.

CHAPTER 32

A MONTH AFTER I'd left Thamkrabok, I still hadn't heard any news from my friends. Then one night I received an upsetting email from *Raphael*. She told me she was back drinking, and that *Oscar* had left her. The despair and sickness was raw in her email. It was only two paragraphs long, but it was enough. It was easy to detect the excuses she was making to herself. I felt so sorry for her, but knew there was nothing I could do to help. What could I say? I couldn't blame *Oscar* for leaving her, and I just felt sad for them both. He obviously loved her but he needed to protect his own sobriety.

I replied to her email and told her I thought she needed to get back on track. There was no reason for her to spend years wasting her life as a drunk. It was obvious she wasn't enjoying her return to drinking so she should just stop again. There was no point in dwelling on her relapse—she had to look forward. She mentioned that she had sent an email to Phra Hans, and I agreed that this was a great idea. I sent her all my best and really wished I could do more for her. I sent the message and was dismayed to receive a message in German informing me that my email hadn't been delivered. I tried to re-send the email a few more times but had no success. I felt terrible and hoped she didn't think I just wasn't bothered emailing her back.

Raphael's email served as a stark reminder of how fragile my sobriety could potentially be. I had believed that all of us at the temple would beat our addictions, and that the temple programme was a sure way to quit for good. I had forgotten Phra Hans' warning that Thamkrabok could not get us sober, but could provide the tools to make it easier for us to do it. At the end of the day the effort to quit would need to come from inside ourselves.

I felt awful about what had happened to *Raphael* for days afterwards. The last time I saw her at the temple she had seemed healthy and positive and ready to live a wonderful life. That was all gone now and the healthy *Raphael* might never get a chance to come back again. I really hoped she'd be okay. I know from experience that there's not very much other people can do to stop an addict who wants to drink or use. *Raphael's* future was in her own hands. All I could do was try and learn from her mistake, and remind myself that a return to alcohol would be a return to misery and depression. I had never met anyone who had returned to drinking after being sober and claimed that they were glad they did it. They might have been full of justifications as to why they drank again, and have a list of people or situations which drove them to it, but at the end of the day these stories were always full of regret.

THE FIRST COUPLE of weeks of sobriety were an emotional rollercoaster. I had been hiding my emotions behind chemicals for years but now they were all out in the open and I felt very raw. I could be completely ecstatic one minute and in floods of tears the next. Nevertheless, it was great to have my emotions back again and I felt really alive for the first time in a long while.I began to see the world in a whole new light and I was glad to have been given a second chance at life.

On a trip to a popular seaside resort in Thailand a few months later, I passed a clinic that offered blood tests. It had been four years since my liver had been checked and I'd been told that it was being damaged by my excessive alcohol intake. I had no idea where things stood now. I needed to know, but was afraid of what I might find out.

I'd had mild abdominal pain around this time, but it was nowhere near as bad as when I'd been drinking. I knew this pain could be due to other factors, but I still worried about my liver. Standing outside the clinic, I made a pledge to myself that no matter what the outcome of the test was, I would not drink again. I enjoyed my life too much now to want to destroy it again, and I vowed that even if it turned out that my life expectancy had been reduced, I would spend whatever time was left to me sober. I owed that much to myself, and to Oa who had stuck by me through my addiction. I took a deep breath, and went into the clinic to take the test.

I had come to the resort to unwind but I found it difficult to relax as I waited for my test results. It had seemed so easy when I had decided to take the test, but now my mind was wavering. Would the test results really not make a difference to my decision to quit alcohol? Would there be any point in remaining sober if the news was bad and I found out I was going to die soon? On the other hand, if the results showed that my liver had healed, maybe I could get in a few years of drinking before things got bad again. These were the thoughts going through my mind as I waited for the results, and they really frightened me. I worried that I might lose my resolve to stay sober and I knew that if I did, I would lose everything.

As time wore on, however, sanity prevailed and the answers to my questions came easy. No matter what the results from the blood tests were, I knew I would remain sober—I wouldn't wish the life of a drunk on a dog.

I spent a restless night thinking about life and death, and all the years I'd wasted as a drunk. I have discovered over the years that my life became better when I tried to do the right thing. 'Do good and good things happen' seems to me to be the rule of life. My *satja* vow to remain sober seemed to be taking me where I needed to go, so I decided to relax and enjoy the ride.

I returned to the clinic the following evening with my resolve firmly in place. The results were normal—what a relief! That didn't mean that my liver hadn't been damaged, however, and I wasn't quite out of the woods yet, but it was certainly a good sign and it gave me a real sense of optimism. I silently gave thanks to the monks of Thamkrabok for helping me to get sober, and for providing me with the medicine which I feel certain had helped to heal my liver.

It felt like I had been given a second chance at life, and for this I was really grateful. I doubted whether there would be any more chances and I knew I needed to seize this one for all it was worth and to really make the most of my life. I was still young enough to have a good life and to make up for all the previous wasted time. I wondered what my friends from the temple were doing with their lives, and whether wonderful things were occurring for them too.

THE CLAIM THAT relapse is a natural part of the recovery process from addiction, is probably the least helpful thing I have ever heard from people who were trying to help me. As an addict I was only too happy to latch on to this as an excuse to continue drinking. I would rationalise my pathetic life by telling myself, 'Of course I'm back drinking, it's a normal part of recovery.' I know many people who tell addicts this are well-meaning, and that they are trying to make addicts who have relapsed feel better about themselves so they don't just give up on their recovery, but I hate this statement. Just because addicts frequently relapse doesn't make it a normal part of recovery. If anything, it's the complete opposite. Plenty of people give up addictions without any need to relapse and this should be the aim of any attempt to walk away from addiction.

CHAPTER 33

A LITTLE OVER a year after leaving the temple, the greatest gift of my life arrived. Oa, who was now my wife, woke me up at about 3am. It took me a few seconds to realise where I was, and even longer to understand why I was being woken up in the middle of the night. Her waters had broken! She had no labour pain, but her waters were definitely broken.

I had no idea what to do. Despite all the planning, I wasn't prepared for the actuality of the event. I desperately scanned my memory for anything I might have learned during my nurse's training which would help me now. However, all knowledge seemed to have evaded me—at least, anything that was relevant. Her waters breaking without any labour pain seemed strange to me and I was worried that something might be wrong. I didn't want to say anything to Oa, but I was terrified there might be a problem with the baby. I tried to hide my fear by focusing on a mantra I'd learned at Thamkrabok. It helped me to focus and stopped me from having a total panic attack.

I telephoned the owner of the house we were renting, as he had already offered to give us a lift to the hospital when the time came. There was no way Oa would be going to the hospital on the back of my motorbike!

Our landlord picked up the phone almost immediately and didn't seem to mind being woken up. He had done the same thing for Oa's sister years before when she had gone into labour. This was part of Thai village life—if you had a jeep you were expected to help out your jeep-less neighbours. He was at our door before too long. I was trying to stuff things in a bag for Oa but I couldn't think of what she was going to need so I just threw in a few things that were near at hand. We didn't have time to be choosy. Oa was soon in the jeep and off to the hospital. I locked up the house and followed behind on my bike.

As I rode the bike through the dark night my mind was full of hopes and fears. I hoped that everything would be okay and that when I returned to the village, it would be as a father. I had often pictured how Oa's labour would go, but I never imagined that it would be as confused and chaotic as this. I soon caught up with the landlord. He was moving too slowly for my liking, and I hoped that he wasn't deliberately wasting time. Apparently he had done this with Oa's sister when she was in labour, because he thought it was very lucky to have a baby born in his car. I hated not being in control and willed him to drive faster.

We eventually arrived at the hospital, not a moment too soon as far as I was concerned, and I tried to hurry

Oa along to the maternity section. As usual, however, she moved at her own pace and would not be rushed. The hospital staff said that Oa's burst waters were perfectly normal and that she would soon be having the baby. This really surprised me because she was still not having any labour pain, and I hoped the nurses weren't trying to hide the fact that something might be wrong with the baby.

They directed us to a bed, and I felt so sorry for Oa who only had me for company because I didn't think I was being much help. I suggested that we call her mother and was relieved when Oa's mother and older sister finally arrived. The labour pains were by now quite intense and Oa was screaming the ward down. Unlike what I had seen back home, breathing techniques didn't seem to be such a big deal in Thailand and Oa hadn't learnt any.

Eventually the time came to take her into the delivery room and I was devastated to find out that I wouldn't be allowed to attend the actual birth. I had really wanted to be there when my baby entered the world, and to make sure that Oa was okay, but they just wouldn't allow it.

After what seemed like an eternity, a nurse appeared with a baby boy wrapped in a blanket and she laid him down on the bed. I looked at my son for the first time and fell completely and totally in love with him. I suppose this is how most parents feel, but I had never experienced anything like it in my life. Lying helpless before me was the little man who was going to change my life completely. I knew that nothing would be more important than his needs. Just looking at him was the happiest moment of my life and everything else in the world seemed insignificant.

I wanted Oa to be there with me, but she hadn't yet returned from the delivery room. I was joined in the room by Oa's mum who was just as excited about the new addition to the family as I was. I asked her about Oa and she smiled reassuringly and told me that everything was okay. I felt so relieved. The whole experience had been so surreal that I hadn't yet grasped the enormity of it all. Oa's mother and I spent the next few minutes staring at the new baby. I was completely dumbstruck and all I could do was grin foolishly.

Oa joined us at last and everything fell into place. She was exhausted and could initially only manage a feeble smile. I showed her our baby, and she was just as smitten as the rest of us. Her family and other well-wishers from our village soon arrived in the room and there was a real party atmosphere.

I stayed in the hospital with Oa that night. This was quite usual in Thailand and I was glad to get some privacy. It was strange spending so much time in close proximity to my in-laws. Over the next few days we had hardly a minute without them. I was used to seeing them regularly as we lived in the same village but it was always for short durations. This was the first time we had been thrown together in such an intense way and it was a great test of my sobriety!

The first night in the hospital provided very little in the way of sleep, which was good preparation for the weeks to come. Timmy soon found his voice and he had quite a roar on him. I discovered he liked it when I carried him for a stroll and we got into the routine of moving around the hospital. We got some strange looks as people stared at the unfamiliar sight of a '*luk kreung*' baby: half-Thai and half-European, but I didn't mind the curiosity and was very proud of my son. I must have walked around the hospital with him hundreds of times, but I didn't mind one bit. I just loved being with my child.

Timmy's arrival had changed the focus of my life completely and I was completely happy with this. I had always put myself first, but now this little man was my priority. In spite of all my previous fears and reservations the arrival of my son felt completely right and, now that he was here, it would be unimaginable for life to be any other way.

I USED TO fantasise about being able to travel back in time. I'd want to return to a time when alcohol was still fun for me with little consequences from indulging in it. Or better still, travel back even further to a time before I started drinking and completely change my history—not allow myself to drink in the first place. How different life could have been. However, now this fantasy of time travel no longer appealed to me, because the only place I wanted to be was with my wife and son.

I didn't want to miss a second of Timmy's childhood, and I decided that the long trips back to Ireland were finished. I didn't want to be away from my son for months at a time.

On my first day in Thamkrabok, Phra Hans had promised me that my path in life would find me and it certainly felt like everything was falling into place now. I had no urge to run away and try again somewhere else, because I had finally found where I wanted to be.

In my younger years I had wanted to someday become a father, but later I just didn't feel worthy of it, and I had stopped seeing it as a possibility. Yet now it had happened. A great life was starting to open up for me and it was all falling into place just like the monks at Thamkrabok had said it would.

It HAD ONLY been 14 months since I rode my motorbike away from the monastery to start a new life, but so much had changed. I could never have imagined how good my life could be, and I am still excited at the thought of what the future might bring. In the past, I often went to bed hoping not to wake up again. I am now living my life with purpose, away from addiction, and feeling confident that my new path in life will lead me to discover many more good things.

AFTERWORD

I HATE IT when my mobile phone rings during the middle of the night. It is always either a stranger looking for somebody I don't know, or it is a member of my family phoning with bad news. When my phone woke me before dawn that morning, I somehow knew it wasn't a wrong number. My birthday had been the previous day and it had gone by without a call from my father. We had our bad days, but this was the first time he had failed to give me his best wishes on my birthday. I couldn't care less about birthdays, but they were special to him, and his failure to call left me uneasy, and feeling a little bit annoyed.

Even after getting sober, my relationship with my father had remained strained. Each phone call with him seemed to leave me in a bad mood for hours afterwards. Not because of anything he said particularly, but because of the anger inside me that I just couldn't let go of. On more than one occasion, I promised myself I would stop taking his calls.

The fact that I lived in Thailand and he lived on the other side of the world didn't help our relationship. Absence may make the heart grow fonder, but old hurts still remain.

When my son was born I hoped it would help bring me closer to my father. I worried that my failure to have a good relationship with my dad would be repeated with my own son. I wanted my boy to get to know his grandfather and I knew my father would be a great grandfather because I'd already seen how he treated my niece.

Even though I suspected the news was going to be bad, I wasn't prepared for it. The sound of my sister's distressed voice on the phone unnerved me. My father had suffered a complete heart block while out walking the previous day and had stopped breathing. A passer-by noticed him unconscious and carried out CPR, but he had already suffered a gap when no oxygen had gotten to his brain. He was still unconscious and in intensive care, and the medical team had no idea how much brain damage he had suffered. In fact, they were doubtful he would ever wake up again.

I spoke to the intensive care nurses and asked if I should rush back to Ireland. They advised me to wait for a few hours and see how things developed. When I called back that afternoon the head nurse was more emphatic and told me I should travel back to Ireland quickly if I wanted to say goodbye to my dad. I booked the next flight back to Dublin.

The news completely knocked me for six, and I had no idea how to respond. I felt completely numb and confused as to how to behave. In my drunken days I would have known exactly what to do: Paul would have been inconsolable and everyone would have known about it. During my addiction I would have had my friend alcohol to take the edge off the pain, not that you would have known this by looking at me.

This was the worst thing that had happened to me since getting sober but I refused to drink again. In fact, the thought of drinking didn't even enter my head. I would have said this was a miracle if I'd noticed it at the time, but my mind was elsewhere. I was only concerned with getting home in time to say goodbye. Every time I phoned home to my family the news seemed to be getting worse.

I arrived in Ireland to the news that he was still with us but was now on life support. When I saw him lying in an intensive care unit it came as a huge blow. I had trained as a nurse and worked with critically ill people, and should have been prepared for this sight, but it's not the same when it is your own flesh and blood. My father had always been so independent and strong-willed, but now he looked so vulnerable. His mouth was pulled at a strange angle due to the intubation tube, which only added to his look of helplessness.

Over the next 24 hours my father's condition began to improve and the noise coming from his medical team sounded more positive. We began to hope that he might still wake up. The next afternoon things were going so well they were able to remove his intubation tube. He was now breathing for himself. It felt like a miracle was about to happen and my sisters and I made wild speculations. We hoped maybe he would even be back working in a couple of months. My father was only 60 years of age and if anyone was capable of pulling a comeback it was him. He had left school at 12 and had still managed to become a successful businessman, so who knew what he was capable of achieving.

I was staying with my mother during this visit back to Ireland. We got on a lot better these days, and I now spend a few weeks staying with her each year. On that occasion, she was good enough to give me a lot of space during this visit, and I really needed it. My father's condition obviously came as a shock to her, but she had lost him years before.

My father continued to make improvements over the next few days, but our wilder hopes became tempered by reality. It looked like he was going to survive but it was obvious that there had been a lot of brain damage. For years he had felt like a stranger to me, but now I was a stranger to him. I had only come back to Ireland for ten days and as the time came for me to leave, his progress had already slowed down. With a lot of help he was able to sit up on a chair, and he could speak words but he wasn't making sense.

The damage that occurred to my father's brain during the time his heart stopped is permanent. I returned to Ireland six months later with my wife and son. We visited him but had to leave because he gets upset if there are strangers in the house and that's what I am to him now. My father is completely dependent on other people and this is the life he would have previously dreaded the most, but the person that he was is no more. I am in the peculiar position of wanting to mourn somebody who isn't even dead—a type of limbo.

I HAVE TO face the fact that I will never get to resolve my relationship with my father. Even when I was a drunk, he was always an important part of my life and he remained an important part of my life when I travelled to the other side of the world to escape from everything. Recovery has brought such great joy, but it doesn't mean that everything is going to fall into a neat little resolution. If I have learned anything, I have learned that life isn't like that for people in recovery—it isn't like that for anyone.